SISTREN

BY Iolanthe

GRIFFIN
THEATRE
COMPANY

CURRENT THEATRE SERIES

First published in 2026
by Currency Press Pty Ltd,
Gadigal Land, Suite 310, 46–56 Kippax Street, Surry Hills, NSW 2010, Australia
enquiries@currency.com.au
www.currency.com.au

in association with Griffin Theatre Company

Typeset by Brighton Gray for Currency Press.
Printed by Fineline Print and Copy Services, Revesby.
Front cover shows Iolanthe and Janet Anderson.
Cover photograph by Brett Boardman. Cover design by Paper Moose.

Currency Press acknowledges the Traditional Owners of the Country on which we live and work. We pay our respects to all Aboriginal and Torres Strait Islander Elders, past and present.

A catalogue record for this book is available from the National Library of Australia

Contents

Author's Note

---

consider this proof of life. proof that trans girls and black girls can not only hold an audience, but can grab them by the hand, teach them to ki, imitate them, make them laugh, pop a fart joke in there somewhere and remind you that you are responsible for the collective.

i wrote this because there is nothing more expansive, exciting and expressive than sisterhood. consider this text proof of a full, ridiculous life. so that one day, when real world versions of Isla and Violet are tasked with 'finding themselves' in a library, they can.

<3

All love & respect to: grace jones, tracy chapman, eartha kitt, Kath & Kim, ilana glazer + abbi jacobson, indya moore, solange knowles, toni morrison, ethel cain, erykah badu, billy porter, rihanna, little richard, munroe bergdorf, andré leon talley, michaela coel, SOPHIE, audre lorde, JT, and of course, to all the party girls, dolls, black girls, twinks, gays, fabulous ones and honourary members of the SISTREN universe.

Sistren was first produced by Griffin Theatre Company in association with Old Fitz Theatre at the Old Fitz Theatre, Gadigal Land, Wooolloomooloo, on 26 June 2025, with the following cast:

ISLA	Iolanthe
VIOLET	Janet Anderson

Director, Ian Michael
Production designer, Emma White
Lighting designer, Kelsey Lee
Composer & Sound designer, Daniel Herten
Video designer, TK Abioye
Dramaturg, Dylan Van Den Berg
Community engagement strategists, Janet Anderson and Iolanthe

A Green Door Theatre Company Production

CHARACTERS

ISLA—she/her—black (Afro-Caribbean)—a seventeen-year-old self-proclaimed 'baddie'. Violet's soulmate. From a working-class, single-parent family. Lots of aunties make up her orbit. The youngest of three siblings. She can be described as delusionally optimistic, the type of person who could 'this is all for the plot and the wikipedia page' her way out of the most heinous situations. Aesthetics and optics are very important to this girl. A visual artist and painter, she dreams of her work being witnessed in big 'richy-roo galleries'. Constantly creating—has an ever-growing notes app page titled 'ideas'. A deep, unholy fear of being basic. Gorgeous, obviously.

VIOLET—she/her—white (Dutch and other misc white)—another seventeen-year-old self-proclaimed 'baddie'. Isla's soulmate. From a working-class family. Been on puberty blockers for a year and half. The kind of person who could lead a cult if she wanted to. She could smear dog shit on her face one day, and by the end of the week dog-shit-on-the-face is thee new trend. She lives in such close proximity to Caribbeanness that maybe she's a teensy bit too comfortable with the patois accent. She's razor smart and has devoured enough *RuPaul's Drag Race* to win any trivia, and (almost) any argument. If there's a mirror (or window, or someone else's sunglasses) she looks in it. She dreams of going to Central Saint Martins for costume design, being a runway model for Mugler or running away to the mountains with her future lesbian lover … whichever comes first. She's beautiful, duh!

NOTE

It's important to note that the world these girls live in is the present. In the 'now'. This was written across 2023–24 but was staged in 2025/26, so the 'now' i speak of, is actually an April 2026 kinda 'now'.

As chronically online girls, the characters possess a rolodex of meme references, NeNe Leakes appreciation and Gen-Z slang. They worship at the altar of Tiffany Pollard on *Flavour of Love* and Katie Price's OG makeup looks. They search for examples of themselves in the blue-light of their iPhones. The impact that Rue and Jules' friendship from *Euphoria* provided them is … well, intense. Consider this play to be a distillation of their universe—drenched in soft pinks and lilacs, with erratic leaks of South London rebellion, childhood anxiety, intoxicating bouts of disassociation and chaos.

You might notice the frequency of dissociative 'skits' throughout the work. Consider them to be truck stops in the minds of Violet and Isla. Sometimes there's a clear neurological leap between what happens in 'reality' and the subsequent skit that ensues. Other times the connection is less clear. This is deliberate—these moments reflect the imaginative prowess of their brains. There are boundless playgrounds that sit in their heads, ready to be activated, and this is how it comes to manifest. These scenes have no pressure to give context other than one consistent rule: they always reflect the internal life of the girls. If they are head-to-head beefing in reality, their dissociations will be charged by their emotional lives: off-kilter and fiery. The actors should take up all the comedy glory that they can. Full commitment to the accents and physicality is required.

The world of this play is verrryyyy stylised. There are video-game sound effects that complement their gestures, there are projections that resemble that of Beyonce's Renaissance Tour, and there's pink fluff like … everywhere … I want it to feel like an all-encompassing world that the audience steps into. Like the circus but for cunty girls and gays.

SOUND EFFECTS

Every time the word 'pussy' or 'cunt' is spoken = cat reoowwww

Every time the word 'gay' is spoken = 'GAAAAY'

Every time someone winks = sparkle sound

Every time someone side-eyes = knives slashing sound

NOTE ON TEXT

One final thing … the irregular capitalisation of sentences and lack of formal 'Acts' is mostly due to my resistance to rules and structure. These characters themselves resist regulation, and so did I in creating them, mwah!

This playtext went to press before the end of rehearsals and may differ from the play as performed.

SCENE ONE

Everything goes black. Ideally, the actors enter the stage as inconspicuously as possible. The pulsing sound design brings us in, it's loud. It's almost like the stage is buzzing, throbbing perhaps, with the impending energy. The stage remains black. As the sound peaks, a spotlight (preferably with a pink wash because purrrrr) hits VIOLET. *She basks in the glory. Serves face.*

Elaine Stritch's 'Are you Having Any Fun' plays out and VIOLET *lip-syncs with full choreography. This is about her and the fantasyyyy so let her joy in this moment take as long as it needs to. Eventually, she starts chatting shit—*

VIOLET: [*playfully with the audience*] stop!! stop!!! [*Not-so-playfully this time*] STOP!

…

Soooo …

What are you lot staring at?

I put on a good show, no?

Yeeaahhh I did, don't lie, you were gagging for it.

She singles out an audience member.

you had that look in your eye like 'yesss i'm getting my money's worth outta this show'.

In the following sentence, as she says the words 'two divas', lights flash to reveal ISLA *through a window behind the room* VIOLET *is currently in. A sign above* ISLA *reads 'the other diva in question' as she continues.*

What, you never been locked in a small room with **two divas**, forced to bask in their fabulousness for ninety minutes—no interval? You never been to the fish market?

VIOLET *mimes throwing out a fishing line and spinning the reel. She plays and pretends there's a fish pulling the end of the line.*

Fresh tilapia!!!

She pretends the line is caught in her foot. As though ***she*** *is the fresh tilapia.*

Oh no; it's just me.

She smirks at her ridiculous joke. She notices ISLA *in the backdrop again.*

Don't start making a fuss, she's gotta sign in before she comes in here. Patience is a virtue.

To prepare you, I'd say this experience is on par with … late-night doomscrolling, you know?

Looking at impossibly pretty girls with expansive vocabulary and inherent rhythm discuss the socio-political state of the world, leaving you questioning if anything you say or do will ever be of any importance.

We've all been there. If I were you, which I'm not

She says 'thank god' under her breath.

I might even consider leaving.

She wags her index finger in the air as if to say 'nuh uh uh'.

Just so you know, it'd be really obvious and you'd probably get labelled a big fat racist or a raging transphobe, which really isn't worth the trouble.

So kick back, shut up, and let the professionals hold it down.

The actor must search for an aunty (or uncle if it's an aunty-less audience) in the crowd.

Except for you Aunty, you can do whatever you want, really. Answer the WhatsApp call, see if I care.

VIOLET *notices* ISLA *heading in.*

OooOooHhhHh here comes trouble:) Everybody put your hands together for my third nipple and biological sister, Isla!

In reference to every American talk show ever, ISLA *enters with a little dance routine, Hollywood smile and the support of a canned laughter + talk-show-music soundscape. It's like a very silly but well-oiled machine.*

ISLA: hiiii everyone I'm Isla—

VIOLET: already covered it, babe

ISLA *pulls a stupid face at the audience.*

ISLA: oh! Ohhkay!

VIOLET: [*speaking to the audience with pride*] told you, she's a goodun

ISLA: [*laughing*] shut up, man.

ISLA *makes herself at home in the space. She dumps her bag down, grabs a lipgloss and gets comfy.*

And … ? How have you been going with the whole 'live audience' thing?

VIOLET: Terribly ;)

In the distance we hear the sound of footsteps.

ISLA: Mmm looks like it. So, what else have you covered?

VIOLET: ummm I gave em a show, called myself fishy

**wink.*

and then just basic housekeeping stuff

ISLA: oh so they don't know where we are?

VIOLET: nah I left that for you

ISLA: HA okaaay so right now, yeah, we're waiting in probably thee dingiest, stuffiest, farmer-wants-a-wife-coded office known to man. It looks like the lair of some washed-up stalker on them late-night exposé TV shows.

She does an impression of a corny British TV presenter.

'Today we meet Craig, a sixty-three-year-old predator whose diet consists of mattress foam and digestive biscuits. He hasn't left the house in four months or spoken to a woman in six years.'

You get the gist.

The footsteps get super close. They both prick their ears to hear.

VIOLET: Nooooo

ISLA: Are you mad?? I only just got here! Why are people with the shittest vibes always early? It's too eager, man.

VIOLET: [*to the audience*] she didn't mean that.

The door rattles.

Oh fuck—it's about to begin. [*To the audience*] Drink your drinks now, okay? it gets a bit gross.

She sits down beside ISLA.

Aaaaand, here we go. Oh god.

BOTH: ‘sit down’

ISLA: ‘sit down’ he says, he keeps repeating it

VIOLET: like we ain’t heard him the first time

ISLA: like we can’t see—

VIOLET: and **feel**—

ISLA: the little chunks of saliva he spits every time he finishes the word ‘sit’

VIOLET: like there isn’t a big fuck-off vein pulsing in his forehead, you know the one that pops out when men get really mad?

ISLA: i’m already fidgeting in my chair cuz I have the tendency to laugh in these sort of situations and it really doesn’t do me any favours

VIOLET: I wanna tell him straight-up: ‘we are sat down, Sir’

ISLA: should’ve gone to Specsavers

VIOLET: but I know that’ll only make him madder. Every time I’m in this office I look at the wall behind him. It’s easier than looking at his face.

Pause.

That was mean … but it’s also true. On the wall there are four framed certificates reading

ISLA: ‘Winner of the Royal Public School Award 2019’

VIOLET: I bet you’re thinking, ‘public schools get awards?’ for what, going a whole year without a stabbing? Yes. and we did actually have a stabbing—one of the Year Tens, so it’s [*in a Northern Irish accent*] not funnay!

ISLA: I feel like that deserves a moment of silence.

VIOLET: [*clarifies for the audience*] he’s alive he just won’t have a football career—

ISLA *silences her with a tut. They have a moment of silence until:*

VIOLET *gestures to the wall.*

So from the left we have: 2022

ISLA: 2023

VIOLET: 2024

ISLA: then there’s just a nail stuck into the wall for where 2025 would’ve been

VIOLET: that stabbing I was talking about? Might have something to do with …

She gestures to the nail on the wall.

… just saying!

ISLA: for real, like there's world hunger, a raging housing crisis, genocide across the globe annnnnnd then there's losing the public school award and for some strange reason, everyone acts like they're equal causes

VIOLET: I'm pretty sure he thinks **we're** to blame. Just last week he held a lecture for all Year Twelves called: 'The Curse of Cancel Culture'. It was mandatory for Isla and I and optional for everyone else.

She side-eyes the audience.

ISLA: it's like when I spent the summer before Year Nine in Jamaica and came back with goddess braids down to my arse—

VIOLET: —they were so sexy—

ISLA: —i was **just** about to say that! Thank yoiuueee

In sync the girls do some bestie signifier together as if to say 'period!'

Anyways I was called into his office on the first day back cuz apparently 'braids aren't school uniform'. **Well** I suppressed the urge to tell him 'suck your mudda u fuckin pussyhole'

**cat reeeowww sound effect.*

and rather, kindly redirected him to the picture of his blonde white daughter in Bali on the verge of traction alopecia. According to him, I threatened his 'family unit', go figure.

VIOLET: [*as Mr Glass*] 'i hate to admit it, er—

Pause.

—girls,'

ISLA: you see he always does this weird thing before he calls Violet a girl

VIOLET: it's like he's saying the 'right thing' but signalling that he doesn't agree

ISLA: hairless prick

VIOLET: [*as Mr Glass*] 'There's a lot of potential but this behaviour'—

ISLA: they loooove that word. Potential.

[*As Mr Glass*] 'ISLA ARE YOU HEARING ME? Or am I just speaking into the vooooid?'

VIOLET: Men like this shouldn't use so many vowels. It's very [*in* Kath & Kim *accent*] *déclassé*. Vowels are for girls, non-binary people, furries, and Idris Elba. I don't make the rules.

ISLA: 'yes, sir.' I say. 'I can hear you, it's just—respectfully, I don't think we did anything wrong. The curriculum is really outdated, Sir, I'm not gonna lie. We were using critical thinking skills and a really interesting debate was starting'

VIOLET: [*as Mr Glass*] 'In Food Technology?'

ISLA: 'well, yeah! Isn't that the whole point of being in school?'

VIOLET: [*as Mr Glass*] 'It says here that you called Miss Finney a—excuse my pronunciation … "rassclart murderous witch'?'

Beat.

ISLA: [*exasperated*] ugh well … she's just gone and taken it completely out of context! The fact is that non-organic fruits are filled with so many pesticides, it would actually blow your brian, Sir, if you knew how many—and I just don't feel comfortable with her poisoning the growing minds and bodies of working-class children in the UK!

VIOLET: 'yeah, sir' I chime in—'Isla was just advocating for the wellbeing of the collective. What's the point in having a school if everyone is malnourished and can't think clearly? Also, Lily Mathews was speaking up and she never says anything, can't you see that as progress?'

ISLA: [*as Mr Glass*] 'Sure, Violet, calling staff members 'murderers' is definitely a sign of progress.'

The girls sit with what he just said with stank looks on their faces.

I think he thinks he ate that. and it's just—

VIOLET: embarrassing really

ISLA *looks at* VIOLET.

ISLA: you said that one out loud, V

VIOLET: [*to* ISLA] did I? Well, it is! It's [*exactly the same*] embarrassing really

ISLA: [*as Mr Glass*] 'No, Violet, I'll tell you what's embarrassing. That at three-seventeen p.m. today, after your little sidekick here screamed bloody murder in a children's cooking class, you tweeted 'they really out here putting cyanide in the kool-aid. Health and Safety at St John's Public? They never heard of that. #ISLA4PRESIDENT'.'

Beat. The girls try not to laugh.

VIOLET: you don't understand I literally cannot even look in Isla's direction cuz I'll laugh

ISLA*'s eyes are shut, her lips are pursed.*

They never say this aloud, but their brains are short-circuiting, probably frantically saying something like:

don't laugh,
no
no
Nooooooo
don't you fucking laugh girl,
DON'T laugh,
NO!
!!!!!!!!!!!!!!!!!!!!!
you have all the time in the world to laugh after this
oh god
ohhhhhHHhhhHHhhHHH godDDddddDdddD
oh GOD!

It's too much man!!! They erupt into laughter. They howl and wheeze and chortle. It's inappropriate but damn, can't a girl have a laff?

Now, from a scientific standpoint it's actually really interesting cuz I didn't know a human body could turn that shade of colour. It's giving what I imagine David Lynch's Pinterest board to look like, just pure **red**. He's so mad, it's not like anything we've seen before.

ISLA: He slams his fist on the table and tells us that we have severe behavioural issues

VIOLET: he says in his entire teaching career he's never met kids with less impulse control

ISLA: he labels us a 'lethal combination' which I thought would be a really cute name for our girl group if we were ever to make one, hello! wake it up!

VIOLET: he dismounts his chair and trots over to the filing cabinet in the corner.

As ISLA *says the word 'SANCTION' it reads out in scary red writing on the projector behind her. It's melodramatic.*

ISLA: There's a drawer at the very top which has the word 'SANCTION' written in red Sharpie across it.

VIOLET: Ugh for fuck's sake!

As ISLA *says the word 'SUSPENSION NOTICE' it reads out in scary red writing on the projector behind her. It's melodramatic.*

ISLA: he licks his finger like a pervert before he rifles through it, pulling out two sheets that read 'SUSPENSION NOTICE'

The girls start to panic.

VIOLET: fuck fuck fuck fuck fuck fuck fuck

ISLA: yeah, not gonna lie this is really bad. Like **really** bad. It's just like, the timing's not fab, you know? We only got three more months of Year Twelve and *suspension* really isn't a word my family are familiar with. Meanwhile Violet can't find another word other than 'fuck' in the entire english language

VIOLET: [*to* ISLA] erm, sorry babe, this is just thee worst thing possible right now.

ISLA: [*sarcastically*] yeah I know I'm experiencing the exact same fucking thing

VIOLET: As he starts filling out the 'reason' box on the sheet of paper, he speaks aloud: 'more often than not their incidents include each other'

ISLA: 'egging one another on'

VIOLET: 'constant political correctness'

ISLA: 'relentless disregard for school uniform'

VIOLET: 'resistance of rules'

ISLA: and then, in the 'additional notes' box, he writes **'total separation is required indefinitely'.**

Beat.

Let this moment last as long as it needs to.

They take this in.

VIOLET: he's been talking for such a long time that a thick layer of white foam has formed in the corners of his mouth

ISLA: when he pauses, he licks up the crust and chases it with water. I feel sick. He asks if I even want an education. I'm so pissed off I can't even think of a good read.

VIOLET: he says he 'can't afford to have any liabilities like last year'

ISLA: he points one hand up to the empty spot on the wall

VIOLET: [*as Mr Glass*] 'From this moment onwards you are both suspended for two weeks. If I see you on the school premises I will need to intervene with harsher sanctions. You will no longer be in the same classes. You are no longer allowed to interact nor cause havoc in recreational periods such as break time or lunch or any extra curricular activities.'

ISLA: [*continues as Mr Glass*] 'I'm going to call home and let your guardians know of this sanction and I expect them to enforce the separation at home too. This will continue to the end of the year. Till exam season is over and the school awards have been announced.'

VIOLET: [*as Mr Glass*] 'Is this clear'

Beat.

I say yeah almost instinctively. He smiles at me. I look at Isla and her face looks like a slapped arse. Just full of disgust. He says to her, 'Isla, I asked you if this is clear'

Silence.

I watch her muster up every bit of strength not to yell or cry or laugh or smash something. I forget that I'm even in my body altogether. My legs feel like they're screwed into this chair, like I'm just observing it all.

[*As Mr Glass*] 'Isla I'm going to ask you one more time'

ISLA: M-hmm

VIOLET: [*as Mr Glass*] 'Good. Have a nice weekend. Off you go. And when you come back, I want you in the appropriate uniform'—he nods to my bestie's freshly done acrylics before he continues, 'Now

Violet, I just need you to stay for a few moments. Would you be so kind?'

Beat.

ISLA: Is this guy alright? I'm not tryna leave her trapped in his office after school. I've watched the case files, I know how these freaks think. The worst psychopaths love the prettiest girls. Just saying. So I go, 'I'm happy to stay and wait.' I look at V, then back at him. She looks … funny. Not funny HA HA, funny weird. He nods to her.

Beat.

VIOLET: [*as* VIOLET] 'please just go, Isla'
ISLA: ?
VIOLET: 'please'
ISLA: WHAT???

Beat.

VIOLET: [*quietly*] just go.

ISLA *picks up her bag and leaves.* VIOLET *is left on stage.*

Beat.

The air feels really weird without her here. Stale and cold. A full minute passes.

Beat.

He clears his throat to speak and I can hear the phlegm rattling in his mouth.
[*As Mr Glass*] 'This changes things, obviously.
You know what you need to do.
Nobody will know it, right?' He asks. I say no.
[*As Mr Glass*] 'Promise?' I say yes.
[*As Mr Glass*] 'Your lips are sealed?'

Beat.

I say yes.

Blackout.

SCENE TWO

4:45 p.m. Sounds of car doors, sirens and school kids in the distance. Top room of a raggedy Secondary School in Croydon, South London. I want the room to be a symbol of the girls' state of semi-delusion. It has all the furnishings of a school classroom, except everything (and I mean ***everything****) is fluffy and saturated in feminine colors. Think 'Uzumaki Gallery' set design (look her up online if you must and thank me later).*

There is a large rectangular cutout on the back wall, which doubles as a window (when the girls are in reality) or a meme/TV screen (when the girls are either online or in a skit). Allow the sky to change hues as the play goes on, signifying the passing of time.

In the same way that the room is a glamorised version of a classroom, the girls are wearing glamorised versions of school uniforms, altered to make them 'cunty'. Not gonna lie, it's a classic reference, but Dionne and Cher from Clueless *come to mind as inspiration.*

When the lights come up, ISLA *is trawling through a cupboard on stage, lost in thought. The audience can't see what she's doing. The sound of a rapidly bouncing ball builds in intensity. It's offputting. Scary even. Jolted by the realisation that she's being watched, she closes the doors, the sound stops, and she returns onstage with a canvas and easel.*

ISLA: [*to the audience*] Thoughts??

She waits. No answer. She clarifies:

On the room. Not that previous conversation. I'm so pissed I don't actually wanna know what you think about that.

She inhales sharply. Attempts to change the topic.

So, this is our favourite room in the whole building. It's like the penthouse suite but the Temu version so it's the size of a broom cupboard. It's the furthest from the staffroom, the smoke detectors haven't worked since about 1966

She gestures to smoking and says 'hellurrrr'.

and the windows open onto the roof so you can do a likkle photoshoot moment. Perfect if you wanna text a guy like 'come to the roof right now' and do a little one-two

She does a little dance on the spot to symbolise 'getting freaky'.

and worst-case scenario he's a weirdo and you just push him off. Four storeys, remember?

The sound of a body smacking four storeys of building, and then a dramatic splat sound. ISLA *is peering out of the window as if she's just witnessed the fall.*

White boys fall fastest.

The word 'FACTS' is written across the back wall.

I don't make the rules, it's a law of physics.

Kiddingggg. I actually shouldn't be yapping this much, I have so much overdue shit and here I am talking to you lot. Stupid, man.

D'ya wanna know what I'm painting?

She turns the canvas around and it is an extremely violent painting of a man who looks a lot like Mr Glass.

For context, I used to have recurring nightmares about skinny jeans. I'm not joking. I could be having the most peaceful dream, you know, maybe a little love interest has popped up

She makes an 'aawwwrrrrr' sound as if to say PURR.

and we'd be talking, we got eye contact going on—it's sexy, you know?—and so I'm standing here

She marks the spot.

and he's—you know what, let's just call him Skepta, so no-one's confused—standing righhhht here, okay?

She marks a spot opposite hers.

—And finally he starts walking towards me and, and I get a whiff of his perfume and it ain't no Dior 'Sauvage' it's some androgynous scent with like sandalwood notes which makes me like him even more, **and** we still ain't broken eye contact yet cuz we're locked in, you see.

Beat.

But as he's approaching I'm starting to notice in my periphery

She gestures to his crotch area.

that his torso is like … propped up by these *twigs* and I'm telling myself 'Isla, don't look down, don't do it, you like this guy just stay in the moment, yeah?' But there's something so morose about these poles inching closer and closer to my body that I just let myself glance down real quick quick quick but—

A loud horror-movie scream plays out across the space.

It's too late. The damage is done. Two legs stare back at me, vacuum-packed inside of acid-washed skinny jeans, oh my god he's practically bursting at the seams and it's put me right off, it's like if I took an earring out and just pricked him

She gestures to Skepta's thigh area with an imaginary earring.

right there then he'd go—

Lighting change—we enter the SKIT lighting scheme. The screen at the back shows a balloon losing air and flying through the air, synchronised with that fart-like sound balloons make. ISLA *does a camp 'SKEPTAAAAAAAAAAA' scream, arm outstretched as though he's flying away from her. Lightning crack. Lighting returns to reality and the window is back to the sky.*

Fucking terrifying. Had to go to therapy for it. Well—kind of—my mum made me tell my aunty about it and she basically doped me up on ginger shots and black castor oil and made me paint a whole load of people with skinny jeans on. Exposure therapy—look it up. I ain't never dreamt about skinny jeans again. At most, there have been some individuals wearing [Kath & Kim *voice*] capris in my dream—but they can be cunty

**cat reeeowww sound effect.*

so I let it slide. Also, that's what got me into painting. I never—

VIOLET *bounds in. They both scare the shit out of each other.*

VIOLET: FUCK!

ISLA *jumps.*

ISLA: !!!! SHIT, man you scared me!!!

VIOLET: Jesus Christ, Isla!

Laughs.

Just in here yappa yappa yappa to these lot— [*re: the audience*] if you lose your marbles, Isla, I'm not kidding I'll kill myself because who the hell am I meant to chat to?

ISLA: I dunno, your mum? A therapist? That twink who works the Sephora beauty bar?

VIOLET: Archie? Why are you so fixated on Archie and I?

ISLA: I'm not! I just think it's funny you got such a special bond when you've only known him for like five minutes

VIOLET: once a Twink always a Twink

She salutes the air

we've been through this, it's a pipe—

ISLA: PIPLEINE yes I knowww. Everyone, meet Dr Barb—

VIOLET *has miraculously retrieved a clicker from her costume, and pulls a Madonna mic to her face. She does this in a thick Scottish Accent because why not?*

Violet plays with the idea of her doing a TedX Talk on: 'The Twink-to-Doll Pipeline'.

Thank you, thank you. My name is Dr Barb—

She clicks. The screen flashes with a scary pic of Nicki Minaj when she says the word 'Barb' (we used a vevo screengrab where Nicki dons a pink and blone wig, pink lipstick and is seen freakishly eyeballing the camera).

Before VIOLET *can continue her bit, the entire stage goes red and an intruder alarm sound rings out. Then, a 1.5 speed disclaimer (accompanied by red subtitles of the same disclaimer text) reads aloud:*

'this production does not support the recent commentary by the one Onika Maraj of Trinidad & Tobago. though she may have produced some of the fiercest works of all time, she is behaving a fool. chile anyways—'

Back to the Dr Barb lightscape. On with the show, mwah </3

I'm a senior researcher on gender-fluid identities and the evolutionary patterns of transformation, focused specifically on the beneficiary relationship between the

Click.

'twink' and the

Click.

'doll'. Over the past five years I've raked through research highlighting the commonality between those that currently identify with the 'doll community' having previously been members of the densely populated 'twink community'.

ISLA: you think you're well funny.

VIOLET: I **know** I'm well funny. Soooo … why are you here?

ISLA: Tryna work on this. It's due next week, yeah I KNOW, and obviously i'm not in a position to ask for an extension

She shows VIOLET *the painting.* VIOLET *screams.*

VIOLET: Riiiight. I thought only Haitians did Voodoo?

ISLA: And I thought gays have crystals for that? I got a question for **you**, Violet, why are you having one-on-one meetings with a certified loser?

VIOLET: I wasn't—he asked me to stay so I did. Do you really think I wanted to spend another second with him? NO.

you're gonna need a file to cut them down, yanno

ISLA *realises she is talking about the nails.*

ISLA: fuck him, man. I just got them done. And they were bare expensive too, piss me off

VIOLET *hands her a nail file.*

VIOLET: just file them down and square em at the end

ISLA: Can you believe that?

She mocks him disrespectfully.

'Those weapons on your hands aren't school policy' like why was he looking that hard? He's a paedophile

VIOLET: I—what? Okay he's not a paedophile

ISLA: he is! You can't lie, he's an old man, he shouldn't recognise an almond SNS French tip custom set, it's creepy—

VIOLET: —you can't just call people you hate sex offenders, Isla! You can't just say that! Imagine you go around saying that on the bus or something, you'll ruin his career! You just—

ISLA *scoffs.*

ISLA: —career? Paedophiles have *careers*? very progressive—

VIOLET: —it's not that black and white—

ISLA: Why are you defending him?

VIOLET: I'm not.

ISLA: You are. You're playing devil's advocate for a pervert, Violet. How does it feel to be on the wrong side of history?

Lighting change.

Together the girls dissociate. It's dark—a remnant of Mr Glass's previous powerplay and ISLA*'s recent discovery.* ISLA *plays a Judge Judy (New Jersey accent), calling 'Order! Order!' as the sound of a gavel being hit accompanies her.*

Hello. Order! Order! Violet Endersby, for the crime against the SISTREN Act number two-one-two of defending a paedophile—

VIOLET: there's no evidence of that, your Honour

ISLA: Sustained.

Correction: defending a nasty stinking loser; I sentence you to the wrong side of history.

VIOLET: what? For how long?

ISLA: No parole, sweetie. INDEFINITELY.

The same scary echo effect from before of 'indefinitely' is heard. At the same time, large writing on the back screen reads: INDEFINITELY. Reality begins to enter this world as sounds of a fight breaking out brings us back to school.

VIOLET: Isla! Shut the fuck up!

The girls rush to the window to watch the fight.

Is that? Toby?

ISLA: probably, he's always popping off.

They keep watching. They do some comical 'oooh' 'aaah' 'tssssk' 'upper cut' 'duck' 'yeahhhh dassit tobes' 'change your feet' 'mmmhmmm' 'corrrrr's as if they're geezers watching a Conor McGregor fight.

VIOLET: Orrrrwww! He just smashed him! Did you see that?

ISLA *laughs.*

ISLA: man like Toby!!! Booyaka booyaka

The girls are still craning their necks to watch the fight.

Oiiiiii look! Elliot's literally just sat there watching. He's probably waiting for you. Wants to shout you a likkle Zinger Box on the way home, reowwww ;)

VIOLET: I ain't talking to him no more.

ISLA *rolls her eyes.*

ISLA: Oh here we go.

VIOLET: He got me a fucking *Pandora* ring. Do you know how corny that is? A *Pandora* ring. In rose gold, mind you. Have you *ever* seen me wear rose gold a day in my life?

A sad 'wap wap waoowww' sound rings out.

I'm a silver girl, all you have to do is **look** at me to know that. It—

BOTH: Compliments the ginge—

VIOLET: yeh like HELLOOO?? It's like he thinks I'm one of them girls that'll go *Nando's* with him every weekend or something, and consider that romantic? A build-a-bear teddy with his voice recorded 'sleep well, babygirl' message in it?

ISLA: A little spritze of his Lynx Africa on the teddy so you can smell him at night?

VIOLET: *Yuck!* Nek minute I'm taking frozen fish fingers out of the freezer and calling it his 'dinner'? Please.

ISLA: He'd probably love that

VIOLET: babe, it's his **dream**

ISLA: You are the boujee-est broke person I've ever met.

VIOLET: Camembert cheese is two pounds from ALDI, I mean come on. I'm not asking for much.

ISLA: [*sarcastically*] no no just camembert cheese on the daily, a YouTube premium subscription, lifts to Westfield, a weekend pass to Wireless, a trip to Paris, lifetime supply of Anastasia Beverly Hills—

VIOLET: They say it's the city of love, Isla. Sorry that I have taste.

ISLA *pulls a grinder out of her bag and begins the process of rolling a girl-blunt.*

Oh my god did you bring weed to school?

ISLA: no Violet I just summoned by my ancestors' unlimited weed supply and boop! Here it is:))

VIOLET *instinctively reaches into her bag and proceeds to douse the air in Zara body spray.*

VIOLET: sorry that I don't want to be an accessory in you carting drugs into the school

ISLA: **drugs**? Nah nah nah hold that—I ain't never touched no **drugs** in my life

VIOLET: I mean teeeeeechnically it's an illegal substance, Isla

VIOLET *pulls out her phone and starts searching the question 'is weed a drug?'*

ISLA: oh so it's an 'illegal substance now' but last week in Brockwell Park you had no issues telling everyone that your Dutch heritage is the standalone reason for your smoking abilities—

VIOLET: —shut up and listen to this,

She reads aloud from Google.

'is weed a drug?'

ISLA: show me what site you're looking at—

ISLA*'s eye starts twitching uncontrollably.*

Wikipedia??? You might as well be like: 'hey chat, answer my question that I can easily research independently and let's set the world on fire!'

Just cuz they're here [*hello audience*], don't be acting like I didn't teach you how to inhale prop—

VIOLET: —Errrm you didn't teach me shit! Your aunty taught us **both** that and you know it.

They both laugh.

BOTH: [*fondly*] NANCYYYYY <3

VIOLET: aw we gotta see her soon, is she good?

ISLA: Yeah she's fine, she's actually in Jamaica right now.
VIOLET: Is it?
ISLA: Mm

SCENE THREE

VIOLET: Speaking of, d'ya remember Tom Hanks's son?

Lighting change. VIOLET *does an awfully realistic Chet Hanks impersonation as she breaks into real, unadulterated, patois accent.*

Big up, big up. The whole island massive. It's ya boy Chetena, coming straight from the Golden Globes ya na what I'm saying, me finna father Tom Hanks presenting an award. Soon forward come. Big up, tune in!

Lighting change, back to reality.

ISLA *is stunned, mouth agape, speechless. She looks at* VIOLET *the way ZIWE looked at Chet—bewildered.*

ISLA: whaaaaaa?
VIOLET: Have you not seen it?
ISLA: no
VIOLET: oh! Where've you been?

The unmistakable GRINDR notification sound starts ringing out loud. Both girls just blink at the audience as if to say, 'is that us or you?'

ISLA: [*to* VIOLET] I thought you told them to turn their phones off!
VIOLET: [*Kath day-knight (*Kath & Kim*) accent*] you homosexuals are very déclassé!
ISLA: [*singing*] I'm rolling with the L G B T, I'm rolling with the L G B T. Come onnn, whose trade's on the phone?

She waits for someone in the audience to confess ... nobody does.

anyone?
Violet, just check if it's you

VIOLET *reaches for her phone only to find that it is in fact her that's blowing tf up.*

VIOLET: [*hands up*] Guilty!!
Designer pussoire! Lock me up!

Sound of a jail gate clanging rings out.

ISLA: Nah lock **them** up, man! Going after a kid?

VIOLET *side-eyes to this. She opens her phone and refreshes the home page.* ISLA *peers over her shoulder to look.*

check if you got any matches in here.

The girls' eyes dart from the phone up into the audience, and they go between reading:

VIOLET: zero metres away
ISLA: oH My GoD!
VIOLET: It's like a butcher-shop window in here
ISLA: ewww brother! Ewww! What's thaaaat? What's that brother?
VIOLET: Well yes, it's good to know my target demographic is in attendance tonight:)
ISLA: what, detty pigs?
VIOLET: no … f*ggots, obviously!

Immediate lighting shift to something camp and fabulous. In my silly goofy playwright fantasy I'd love them to do a costume change but that might be too much. A gay anthem plays ... and the girls dance 4 their lives. In a dream world, confetti would rain from above. Very GAY.

They return to reality.

SCENE FOUR

ISLA: MORE messages? Seriously? That must do wonders for your ego, V. I would just sit and let the compliments roll in.
VIOLET: I wish it was all compliments, mostly it's—
ISLA: —wait wait stop! swiping! oh my god!!!! is that Jayden?

Chortles.

I didn't know he was gay!
VIOLET: he's not gay

ISLA: he's on Grindr

VIOLET: [*shady*] just cuz he's tapping me doesn't mean he's gay

ISLA: [*jokes*] no straight man is arching his back for a mirror pic! Look at that, his back's a perfect 'C'! That's a homoseggshahh!

ISLA grabs her phone and runs, trying to record a voice message to Jayden.

Oi Jayden it's Isla, your body is teaaaa bitch!

VIOLET: NO, Isla! STOP!! Delete it!

ISLA: why?? He'll find it funny—

VIOLET: no he won't—please Isla—

ISLA: —he's like family—

VIOLET: —give it back give it back give it back—

A 'sent' sound plays out. Silence falls.

tell me you didn't just do that. No no no no Isla that's not—fuck! Oh my god—I wanna kick off right now, I swear to you—why does she do this? lemme breathe and think of cute things like baby goats—it's sent, you actually sent it?—ack fuck, V, breathe out—I'm gonna box her in the mouth—no, Violet, breathe in—baby goats with ribbons in their hair—sunset at the Eiffel Tower—a fresh bottle of Aesop's Marrakesh Intense—

ISLA: V, relax, it's not that deep just delete it

VIOLET: I can't! This app don't work like that, if it's on his phone it's on his phone—Isla what you just did—you just outed him! And you made me part of it! I'm vexed I can't lie

ISLA: I didn't out nobody, he's got his name all over Grindr with his face firmly attached! If I happen to recognise him, that ain't on me

VIOLET: I—ugh! I can't talk to you about this

—it's not strictly a gay app—

ISLA: —yes it is! And that's a good thing, gay people deserve their own app, Violet! It's a gay app—

VIOLET: —says who?

Lighting shift. ISLA *parodies Pooja when she went on Instagram live that one time and was accused of being on Grindr.*

ISLA: A lot of people are asking me 'Are you on Grindr?' No, I'm not on Grindr! … That's a ghey app! That's a ghey dating app. I'm not ghey. Please! Puhleaaaase. Enufff!

Lighting shift. Back to reality.

see?

VIOLET *just rolls her eyes.*

Genuinely, I find it really sad to deep how many beautiful black gay men live closeted lives. The fact that hiding seems like a more feasible option than being known completely is just … sad, man.

With Jayden it's like he's not hiding, he's not ashamed, he's not scared people will recognise him or men like my brothers or my father are gonna catch him with another guy in the area—or maybe he is and he's still choosing to do so. Either way, I back it.

Isla for gay rights, period!

She begins to do the same gay gag dance but is rudely interrupted by—

VOICEOVER: This is a school closure notice. The library and all recreational courts will be closing in ten minutes. The building will close completely at six p.m. Thank you.

The girls do something like shove their middle fingers upwards, or do a big fart sound as a 'fuck you' to institution.

VIOLET: why do you say 'Father'?

ISLA: ?

VIOLET: Father. It's so formal. You sound like Hugh Grant.

ISLA: that's the most offensive thing you've ever said to me, V. I'd rather you call me a slur.

VIOLET: *Hugh Grant* with a hard 'R'.

ISLA *tries really hard not to give her a laugh.*

soooo, why the fancy language?

ISLA *scoffs.*

ISLA: I can't explain to you why I used that one word, I don't even know mysel—

VIOLET: —I saw him.

ISLA: sorry, what?

Long-ass silence.

VIOLET: I saw him.

Beat.

Did you hear me? I saw him

ISLA: That's not funny, V

VIOLET: I'm not laughing.

Beat.

ISLA: Bullshit

VIOLET: Mum's life. I saw him.

ISLA: where?

VIOLET: Angel Station. Like two weeks ago.

ISLA: HAHA very funny, the devil's alive in Angel station. Not fucking likely.

VIOLET: Isla, I'm being so serious now.

A fair bit of silence. Stillness. ISLA *tries laughing.*

It's not a joke.

ISLA *begins to pace frantically.*

ISLA: Owwwe Violet, what are you saying right now? My head is spinning, man—I—okay

She takes a deep breath.

okay, so you're telling me he's been around for two weeks? Yeah? And nothing? No call, no text, no contact through church … nothing?

Beat.

Oh my god why am I even shocked?

VIOLET: it makes sense

ISLA: No like the bar's **been** on the FLOOR for him, and he's still lacking? And I'm still hurt? Fuck sake!

VIOLET: I'm sorry, Isla

ISLA: You can't say that when you took two long-ass weeks to tell me something really fucking important. You can't lie to me and then be like 'I'm sorry Isla'

VIOLET: I weren't lying, it never came up

Silence.

What? What's that look?

ISLA: nothing! I—i've just heard that from you before

VIOLET: wha?

ISLA: I'm just saying that this has happened before, V! just like it 'neeeeever came up' that you were linking Josh P after school on the regular even tho I fuckin told you I liked him!

VIOLET: oh my GOD not this!

ISLA: yes this!!! You let me look like an idiot for half of Year Ten, telling everyone that when his grandad dies he'll be able to give my children intergenerational wealth! Whole time you were snogging him at TGI Fridays!

VIOLET: [*patronising*] … awwww Isla just cuz you're attracted to someone doesn't mean they belong to you or you're in some monogamous relationship.

ISLA: Why'd you keep saying 'they'? He's a **boy**. His name's Josh! I've literally had eye contact with the bulge in his grey tracksuit!

VIOLET: Okay, J. K. Rowling, I'm just being inclusive! I hate that I'm about to say this, but Joshes deserve rights too.

Lighting shift. Both actors stare out at the audience. It must be clear that VIOLET *is a super-chirpy Californian phone operator (the type of woman to only eat Erewhon) and* ISLA *is 'Josh': a boring, white, seventeen-year-old SoundCloud rapper from Essex.*

ISLA: hello

VIOLET: Hi!!!

ISLA: hi?

VIOLET: Hello!!!

ISLA: … uhm … who's this?

VIOLET: My name is Emily, I'm a sales rep from **claimyourrights.com**, would I be correct in thinking this is Josh [*her annoying Cali accent makes it sound like Jaah-sh*] speaking?

ISLA: … uh … yeah … it's more like … Josh …

VIOLET: Amazing, thank you Josh [*again, she says Jaaaaaah-sh*] that's so valid. Now I have a rights referral here from one *Violet Endersby* from Croydon, London. She's just filled in really basic information, but it says here that you're a … God, I hate asking this but … you're a *man*?

ISLA: uh … like I'm seventeen still so technically … I mean, yeah I'm a man

Pause. The annoying phone operator, Emily, ponders on this phenomenon.

Hello?

VIOLET: Hi!!!! My apologies. Next question, do you identify as …

She almost retches.

please excuse me … *straight*?

ISLA: [*immediately*] Yes

VIOLET: Oh! Jump scare!

Mutters to herself as she focuses on her breath.

okay Emily, use your training … Sir … one final preliminary question … would you happen to be caucasian?

ISLA: uh yeah, my mum's Irish but my dad's Italian though, so it's a bit spicy white innit

Beat. Emily begins to weep in fear.

are—Miss, are you cryin?

VIOLET: [*audibly crying*] I don't know, I feel so stupid! I thought you could be like the first black 'Josh'. Or maybe you're bisexual and you haven't had your awakening yet. But then you said that 'spicy white' thing and I knew, I just knew you're a code red. I'm sorry, I've never declined anyone's rights before but—but—it's not your time, sweetie, okay? [*Sobbing*] you've had the last like twenty thousand years to do what you want, and like what have you done with it? Huh? [*Anger rises*] HUH??? What the **fuck** have you done?

ISLA: … uh … I ran a half-marathon for cancer once—

VIOLET: [*yelling melodramatically*] —IT'S NOT ENOUGH!!! Just FUCK OFF, JAHHHHSHHH!

Lighting change. Back to reality. The girls blink at each other for a sec.

ISLA: what u staring at?

VIOLET: I dunno I just had such a vivid image of you with a short back and sides

ISLA: ew that's so weird

Beat. She catches ISLA *before she sits.*

VIOLET: you wanna know what I said to him?

Beat.

ISLA: You—you—what? You spoke to him?

VIOLET: Well, he recognised me, obviously.

ISLA: How?

VIOLET: Okay, I look different but not that fucking different.

ISLA: no, I wasn't—he's been in for like seven years so I'd be surprised if he even recognised me

VIOLET: Well, seems like he would, so that's good news

Beat.

ISLA: So? What was the conversation? I really need you to break it down for me

VIOLET: Okay, sit down then.

ISLA *sits on the sofa. It almost engulfs her.*

Go on. Take the comfy part then, jeeezus.

So I'm at Angel Station on a Sunday, after dancing. You know how I been dancing at the Finsbury Town Hall now ?

ISLA: no

VIOLET: oh, well it's a recent thing, like maybe like … TWO YEARS AGO?

Silence. ISLA *looks at the audience like: 'am I supposed to know that?'*

I've gotten really good now actually.

She tosses her hair.

Guess who's already in advanced jazz, tap and MT? Me bitch. Step aside, Patti Lupone, your time's up with that big mouth of yours!

She begins to sing some corny Patti Lupone song and breaks the world, entering into the audience.

ISLA: Violet!

VIOLET: Anywayyyyss I'm never in North unless I'm dancing, which is why I was confused to see him. And like, shouldn't he be at Church or something?

ISLA: I don't imagine he'd go church any more, considering.

VIOLET: Yeah, but men do crazy things and still go Church on a Sunday. I feel like if being 'good' and going church meant the same thing, the world would be a very different place.

ISLA: You know what I actually fully agree with you, V. But I do really need you to stick to the story.

VIOLET: Right, shit yeah, so I'm standing at the platform and there's been delays so I'm tryna sit down and wait for the Tube. So obviously I walk up and find the nearest bench, and at the end is this man. And he looks bad, Isla. I'm not gonna lie.

Beat.

ISLA: How bad?

VIOLET: Like BAD, babe. He's stinking.

ISLA *buries her face in her hands.*

And you know what the funny thing is? I can feel him looking at me, like in my periphery, but I'm facing away cuz I don't want no random man being like 'what you looking at??'

She notices ISLA*'s body language.*

—are you okay?

ISLA: yeah I'm just deeping the fact that I'm the girl with the stinking dad.

ISLA *begins to dissociate.* VIOLET *joins her.* VIOLET *plays a Priest at a wedding asking 'Do you, Isla, take this man to be your lawfully stinking dad?'* ISLA *squirms before saying 'yes'. 'Do you, Winston, take this diva to be your lawfully fabulous daughter?' Lighting change. Back to reality.*

ISLA *sighs.*

okay okay so he looks at you, hmm?

VIOLET: You're gonna laugh. He goes 'wagwan sexy'. Just like that.

Pause. ISLA *is too stunned to speak.*

—so he calls me sexy, so I look up, and so does he, and I swear to God my stomach drops because I'm like huh? Winston? And I say his name out loud because I am so baffled. And he is too I think, by the look on his face. He looks like the people on prank patrol after they've been scared—just totally bewildered. Like

She serves 'bewildered'.

And you'll love this, Isla. He started pissing himself laughing. He kept saying stuff like 'Lord have mercy'

ISLA *glances to the audience, a nod to the previous patois debacle.*

and he told me I was quite good looking for a boy.

ISLA: Ooop—he said that?

VIOLET: I mean I don't think he knows much better.

ISLA: That's pissed me off. I'm sorry he said that Violet.

VIOLET *changes perspective.*

VIOLET: Not your fault. To be fair, it would've been quite a surprise. A lot can change in a few years. Different gender, pair of tits and a new name—it's a lot for poor old Winston to take in at once, bless him

ISLA: I'm just gonna wait a sec so you can process what you just said.

Beat.

Bless him? You've got to be joking. You know full well that he is not a 'poor old man', and i know you were being funny but—honestly that kind of language riles me up. It makes him this thing that we should feel sorry for, this poor helpless man who doesn't know right from wrong but that's a fucking lie. That's just women accommodating to his bullshit cuz really, let's be real, h—he's—just another statistic. Literally so unoriginal in his bullshit that he went with the same fucking story that every other guy does.

VIOLET: [*in a cowgirl voice*] Whoaaa Nelly Whoaaa Nelly!

ISLA: yeah I know I'm ranting but like come on? I don't give a fuck if this **useless** ass government decides he did his time and paid his dues, what about us? What about his family who know how crazy this man actually is? Sorry but he can't be that remorseful if he gets out and doesn't even bother to let his daughter know.

Is there a world where I can be mad at him, just pure fucking mad at him for:

one, being an actually shitty person and

two, forcing me to be the stereotype.

D'you know how embarrassing it is when people ask me about where my dad is? And then I gotta stand there and watch them, in real time, play a guessing game of what crime he may have committed and how long his sentence is and whether he's ever dropped the soap.

Not to mention the fact mostly, Violet, I'm mad at the system that isn't interested in him becoming a better human or being remorseful, they just benefit from filling prisons with black people. It's not about moral integrity. And then, just as I'm about to defend him with my fucking prison abolition TED Talk, there he is: posted up, stinking at random stations across London. Coming for my best friend. How embarrassing. He can fuck off.

Silence.

Sorry.

Beat.

VIOLET: you ate that
ISLA: really?

VIOLET *pretends to be holding a plate. An imaginary plate that* ISLA *just 'ate' off.*

VIOLET: bestie you licked the plate clean.

VIOLET *pretends to shake the imaginary plate upside down.*

See that?

ISLA *comes to check on the imaginary plate.*

ISLA: No crumbs.

Pause.

I can't believe I'm even asking this but, where'd he go?
VIOLET: ?
ISLA: Like he said wagwan and then he recognised you but then what?
VIOLET: I dunno, my Tube came so I said bye and got on it [*compare-the-meerkat-dot-com style*]

Silence.

Whyyyy do I feel like that was the wrong answer?

Beat.

ISLA: did you take a picture of him?

VIOLET: [*sarcastically*] oh yeah I did actually

ISLA: violet be serious—

VIOLET: —it's so funny you should mention it. Yeah we took a quick selfie right after he called me a man, you know, lightened up the mood

ISLA *is crushed. It was futile hope, but still.*

don't be a baby. Ain't you glad he's out and thriving. Well, not thriving, but he's out at least.

ISLA: describe him to me, V.

VIOLET: are you serious? I can't be arsed to think that hard right now

ISLA: please.

VIOLET: okay but you gotta do something for me—fix the parting at the back of my head or summat

ISLA: aight come den

VIOLET *shuffles over to* ISLA, *and sits between her legs. She takes her hair out of a ponytail and allows* ISLA *to get to business.* ISLA *parts the hair down the middle and starts.*

VIOLET: He looked the same as he always did. Same eyes, big and dark, like yours but bigger. His skin was all dull and ashy. He looked like he ain't had a lick of moisturiser in years, man. I should've just taken the Charlotte Tilbury out of my bag and given it to him, right then and there.

ISLA *scoffs.*

ISLA: don't think that's his style, really

VIOLET: don't know if he deserves a gift really … To be fair though, he seemed like … a lot older

ISLA: older. That's interesting. He ain't that old in the first place.
Do you think he was okay? Like in the head?

VIOLET: I dunno, seven years inside would fuck with you.

ISLA: Mmm.

Beat.

Violet, do you remember about … about?

VIOLET: What, that day? Of course. Never been so scared in my life.

ISLA: I'm sorry.

VIOLET *shakes her head as if to say 'omg not your fault'.*

VIOLET: nah I'm glad I was there with you. All I remember was seeing him grab my Sylvanian Family bakery and

She motions to smashing it against a wall.

DOOSH.

ISLA: not the bakery as well, that one was so expensive! Tuh!

She thinks for a beat.

we stopped playing with dolls after that, d'you remember? Damn, I never thought of that as why we grew up so fast.

VIOLET: [*lightens the mood*] got us started on the hard conversations earlier, though, I'll give him that.

They chuckle.

ISLA: He didn't—like—you know, mention me or Mum, did he?

VIOLET *is obviously made uncomfortable by this.*

VIOLET: [*quietly*] don't make me answer that.

Long, and I mean really fucking long silence. The girls squirm in this quietude. They don't know what to do. Usually, they'd joke about it but they can't find the humour right now. Fuck.

ISLA: [*kisses her teeth*] Honestly, he's a wasteman.

SCENE FIVE

Lighting shift. Thank God—an impetus for some comic relief. The word 'WASTEMAN' is written across the back wall. The girls parody the idea of a 'wasteman'—what does it mean to be both a waste and a man? They give two examples. ISLA *is giving insufferable nepo-baby, Oxford University, trust-fund-having, finance graduate (Boris).* VIOLET *is serving Aryan Gold Coast bloke who has recently purchased a caravan in the hopes of miraculously becoming more interesting (Hugo). Both of these 'men' have freakishly impenetrable egos. They chat up an unseen girl.*

VIOLET: [*to Boris*] arrghhh farrrk bro— [*to girl*] scuse me, can I just say, your energy is *intoxicating*

ISLA: yah yah yah so sorry to bother you, but is that bell hooks you're reading? No waaay I love him—

VIOLET: yeaaaaah it's funny you should ask, yeah I just did a couple days at a silent retreat so I'm suuuuper-sensitive to people's chi at the moment—

ISLA: what's this? Oh darling this is Ralph Lauren everything. I styled it with boat shoes so yeah yeah—

They lean in to hear the unseen girl.

VIOLET: April? Your name's April?

ISLA: oh spectacular month, April, there's a winter chill but an autumnal—

VIOLET: Gemini? No—Virgo—no fuck, Taurus, right? Are you a Taurus?—

ISLA: I go skiing every April, perfect season for the slopes, seriously—

VIOLET: me? I'm a motivational speaker, yeah, mostly chatting shit about masculinityyy—

ISLA: aha so I'm an investment banker, yeah yeah—

VIOLET: I also live in a caravan so I make really sick vanlife content—

ISLA: my dad? aha I mean he does participate in the rape of Africa but like aha—

VIOLET: nah nah nah I can't talk to that, I like to stick to the stuff I **know**, so like, the boys, the Gold Coast and like

She gestures some elusive orb.

energy

Lighting shift. Back to reality. VIOLET *is aware of* ISLA *and her discomfort from the previous conversation. They look at each other, unsure what to do without the shared game.*

You okay? I feel like I should—

ISLA: I'm fine, what do you mean? I'm literally fine.

ISLA *rifles through* VIOLET*'s bag, clearly looking for something in particular.* VIOLET *watches her.* ISLA *makes a face at* VIOLET *for watching her, then goes back to searching the bag.*

VIOLET: Anything I can help you with?

ISLA: Nope, like I said, I'm all good I—here it is—

ISLA *pulls out a pack of cigarettes. She pulls one out for herself, and offers* VIOLET *one.*

VIOLET: Oh, one of my own ciggies, how kind of you <3

VIOLET *lights* ISLA*'s for her. They sit in silence for a bit.* VIOLET *smokes like she's been doing it for years,* ISLA *clearly hates the taste of tobacco.*

You don't have to if you don't w—

ISLA: like it. It's—it's yummy, see? delicious.

VIOLET: What about the YouTube series you made about the negative impacts on your teeth and your skin?

ISLA: You need to learn to separate the art from the artist, V.

ISLA *chokes on the cigarette. She really hates it.*

Okay can't lie, that shit is horrible. Nasty. It tastes like ass!

VIOLET *side-eyes* ISLA *for this comment. Cue the side-eye slashing-knives sound.*

How comes you look so chic doing it? Like your mum?

VIOLET: leave my mum outta this! U know she's quitting innit

Laughs.

my god, every time we go corner shop she keeps saying to the guy 'Marlboro's my toxic boyfriend that just keeps coming back to ruin my life'. She's too much, man. She just exploits his kindness cuz he recognised her from a few episodes of *Coronation Street* back in the day, thinkin she's famous.

ISLA *puts* VIOLET*'s cigarette out dramatically. Beat.*

Can't lie, I been meaning to ask you, what's your new vice?

ISLA: Huh?

VIOLET: if you quit tobacco and weed is 'not a drug', what replaced the arm thing?

ISLA: What arm thing?

VIOLET: I saw you stopped picking your arms like a year ago. And you've been smelling like weed ever since. I figured you moved on to bigger and better things.

Lighting shift. Back to Judge Judy skit—

ISLA: Hello. Order! Order! According to the SISTREN Act number four-one-seven-A, for the crime of stalking your gorgeous best friend, I sentence you to sixty days cigarette rehabilitation.

VIOLET *lets out a camp scream, inhibited by smokers cough, similar to* ISLA*'s 'SKEPTAAAA' scream from before*

VIOLET: NoooooooooOOooooOOoooo!

Lighting change. Back to reality. ISLA *winks at* VIOLET.

You're avoiding the question

ISLA: What even is the question? Did I stop picking my arms? Yes. Good observation.

VIOLET: Why?

ISLA: Why do you care?

VIOLET: tell me
Tell me
Go onnnnnnn
Omg you can't start having secrets now

ISLA: Fine! Whatever! There's no shame in it. My mum paid for laser for me.

VIOLET: Laser? What, on the scars?

ISLA: scars? What scars?

VIOLET: I dunno I thought you were picking at your skin, sooo there'd probably be scars, right?

ISLA: What scars are you on about? I was picking my hairs, obviously.

Beat.

VIOLET: How'd she pay for it?

ISLA: Afterpay innit

Beat.

VIOLET: What hairs?

ISLA *shoots her an angry look. Cue the side-eye sound.*

?

ISLA: The long black ones on my arms

VIOLET: I fully don't remember you having hairs on your arms

ISLA: [*angrily*] Please tell me this is some shitty joke of yours

VIOLET: I—no I'm not joking? Why are you mad right now?

ISLA: You actually do not get to sit there and tell me you don't remember those fucking hairs. Are you being for real?

This is weird.

You were the one who had to point them out in the first place! I didn't have an issue with what my arms looked like until you so kindly had to tell me they were ugly!

VIOLET: I never said they were ugly

ISLA: Okay fair, you didn't. What you actually said was 'monkey hairs' but you know, same difference

VIOLET: I—no—I don't think I woul—

ISLA: Nooooo what we're not gonna do is rewrite history right now, Violet. don't cap. It's literally burnt in my brain.

We're in your room, and we gotta be like eight or something. You were showing me how if you hold a torch behind your hand it glows red. And you do it to my hand, and then you do it to my arm, and then you notice that my arms have all these hairs on it. And you show me that your arms don't, yours are practically naked and like clean, and mine aren't.

And guess what? You laughed and you said, 'Isla you got monkey hairs on your arms'. It wasn't even cruel, the tone in your voice. It was like it was the most obvious thing in the world. You did.

Beat.

VIOLET: Well, laser isn't a very feminist thing to do, Isla

ISLA *scoffs.*

ISLA: Okay.

VIOLET: Are you seriously going to place all of that guilt on me?

ISLA: Why can't you just say 'yeah my bad, I'm sorry I mocked you with one of the oldest insults in the history books. I take it back'.

VIOLET: Because I didn't? I was eight? You can't hold my eight-year-old self accountable to a fucking social construct, Isla. You just have to accept that random shit happens

ISLA: Actually it doesn't. Random shit doesn't 'just' happen. There is no 'coincidence'. No way in which an eight-year-old child can say bigoted shit without it having a link to something bigger. I ain't sayin you're evil, I'm just sayin you projected some fucked-up shit on me. And it took a really long time to heal, a lot of hours plucking my arms, a lot of pain, and a lot of money on laser, fuck!

VIOLET: This isn't philosophy, Isla. Just admit that any form of hair removal is directly playing into this male fantasy that women are fully shaved and basically look like a fucking child! Don't you find that weird?

ISLA *goes to get defensive but—*

I probably said that shit to you because I was repeating the rhetoric that men spit about women. I was just as victimised by misogyny as you were. The difference is, you actually did the whole cosmetic and financial commitment to be desirable for men and THAT isn't feminist. Could never be **me**.

ISLA: [*sarcastically*] so you would never alter your appearance to look more feminine? okaaaaaay

VIOLET: —

ISLA: you literally made me have a ceremony with you when you shaved your legs for the first time. You made me do a lunchtime campaign for your right to HRT.

VIOLET: that's completely different and you know it.

ISLA: is it?

VIOLET: that was so I could have a hope of passing.

ISLA: Have you ever considered that me lasering my arms made me feel more like a girl too, not some old-ass woman? Or an animal even?

VIOLET: Your womanhood wasn't up for questioning! You were a hairy woman before and a hairless one after—either way you were a woman. I didn't get that. I shaved my legs and felt affirmed in my gender. You lasered your arms and felt pretty.

ISLA *kisses her teeth. She doesn't reply nor look at* VIOLET.

We're not the same, Isla. Like Mr Glass said.

ISLA: Huh? Mr Glass?

VIOLET: We're. Not. The. Same. If you do one thing, and I do it too, it isn't gonna play out the same for us.

ISLA: like if you call the police versus if I call the police?

VIOLET: that's not what I'm talking about

ISLA: hmm.

so lemme get this straight. According to you, if I were to get a BBL you'd say it's anti-feminist but if you got one you'd say it's gender affirmation?

VIOLET: probably yeah

ISLA *draws out her argument on the whiteboard behind her. It's giving school chic.*

ISLA: [*bursting into laughter*] that's the dumbest thing I've ever heard! A white woman modifies her body to look black and all she's gotta do is pull out the T girl card and she's in the clear? But if a black girl does it it's not feminist? Make it make sense

VIOLET: what if this hypothetical T girl isn't getting surgeries to look black per say, but as feminisation surgery in order to pass as cis. A BBL is arguably one of the most intense cosmetic surgeries because of how much it alters your appearance. Some T girls crave the safety of big childbearing hips and a tiny little waist so when she gets on the Tube, at peak hour, filled with men in suits, she can actually have a peaceful fucking journey because her silhouette affirms her gender and nobody is gonna out her!

ISLA: it's not really relevant whether T girls are tryna get affirmation, because ultimately it's appropriation

VIOLET: I could argue that a lot of the current beauty trends are coined by queer people—bleached eyebrows? That's drag one-oh-one. Lashes? Thank you, showgirls.

ISLA: —and black girls—

VIOLET: —lace-front wigs? That's queer—

ISLA: —and black—

VIOLET: —Even Beyoncé's *Renaissance* album

The iconic 'UNIQUE' booms out from the heavens. Maybe the girls acknowledge it. Maybe not.

That's ballroom community down—

ISLA: —and black community—ballroom community intersects with the black community and the black community intersects with the queer community

VIOLET: so we always been together?

ISLA: yuhhh babe!! It's written in the stars

VIOLET: That's cute for us. Come here.

The girls hug. They clock the audience staring at them. At the very same time they snap 'what you lookin at?'—Can't take the South London outta these girls. They laugh about their in-sync aggression.

ISLA: Makes me grateful my boobs grew real quick

VIOLET: [*scoffs*] you're too much, man, out here chatting bout my first day as a woman ceremony and not even remembering your C-cup ceremony, wooooowww

ISLA: First of all, it was a cultural ceremony. My aunties say that real Caribbean women are shaped like a capital 'P'—big tiddies, flat body

She gestures while speaking on it. VIOLET *does too because she's heard this theory soooooooo many times.*

Plus, my C-cup ceremony was basically a public vote tho, you can't lie!

VIOLET: watchu mean?

ISLA: I meannnn it was you who gagged when I came to the Year Eight swimming carnival with my tiddies popping outta that one-piece.

VIOLET: oh my god you looked fab. Can't lie, I thought you must've popped some oestrogen before you came, you looked **that** fish.

She thinks for a moment.

Ugh, you know my C-cup ceremony is still pending, I just gotta raise the funds first

ISLA *laughs.*

ISLA: yeah I don't envy you bitches! Having to do up GoFundMes just to afford half of this juiciness!

Beat.

VIOLET: Are you serious?

ISLA: Dead serious bitch. It's a cruel world. I'm out here bouncing, bouncing, black eye, black eye, every time I walk while you're out here serving boy bod! [*In a silly voice*] I do not envy you, baby!

ISLA *turns to face* VIOLET.

[*Defensively*] your words not mine!

Beat. It's like soooo fucking awkward now.

VIOLET: What the fuck? not you gatekeeping womanhood!

ISLA: omg not you being incapable of taking a joke? Violet, be for real you know you're gorg, you're just not giving body like me <3 and that's okay! You give face. You give silhouette.

VIOLET: Shanice, your mouth is moving a lot like a RAT. YAPPA YAPPA YAPPA. Shut it please.

ISLA: not everyone's a descendant of Betty Boop baby—

VIOLET: SHUT THE FUCK UP.

SCENE SIX

Lighting shift to another skit. They take turns in performing the iconic Tiffany Pollard monologue. May the show's director please divvy up this monologue however works best given the established context + tension in the 'real life' world. It should feel like the cutaways in reality TV when people's interviews comment on the fight at hand.

VIOLET + ISLA:

'Pretty much I would let Gemma know that she is a fat cunt
and, um the shoes that she gave me were
not something that I would particularly buy for myself.
They were old maiden type of shoes, and
she said that those shoes were meant to
be worn on a beautiful woman.
So if that is the case she should have put
them back on the rack and she should
never even purchased them because she
was UNQUALIFIED to own those shoes if
that's the case and, um I think that Gemma is just a
disgrace. She's a disgrace to women who are
actually beautiful and classy and, um she
just doesn't have the vernacular she thinks she possesses.
Somebody lied to her several times and told her that she was fly,
hot and sexy
and beautiful and she's nothing like that. She's nothing of the sort'

This skit is violently interrupted by a teacher entering the room. In sync, both the girls' heads snap to look at the door. Lighting shift. VIOLET *and* ISLA *inform the audience of this new presence in the same way they did when they were in Mr Glass's office.*

ISLA: [*whispers*] *SHIT!*

VIOLET: fuck fuck fuck fuck fuck fuck

ISLA: oh god … so basically a teacher—

VIOLET: —Mrs Bexeley, one of the A-Level Art tutors—

ISLA: —has caught us—

VIOLET: —mid Tiffany Pollard impersonation—

ISLA: [*to Mrs Bexeley*] Hi Miss! How are you?

VIOLET: —nice cardigan!—

ISLA: [*to* VIOLET] why the fuck would you say that? That sounded so sarcastic

VIOLET: [*to Mrs Bexeley*] Oh! Sorry I don't mean that sarcastically!

ISLA: [*as Mrs Bexeley*] 'I sure hope not. This is original Marks and Spencer cashmere, very highly sought-after.'

She pats herself down with pride, bless her.

[*As Mrs Bexeley*] 'Anyhoo, I must ask your names, year group and reasoning for being here.'

Beat.

[*To audience*] Look, sometimes a bitch finds herself between a rock and a hard place and she just gotta squeeeeeze her way out of it in whichever way she deems fit.

VIOLET: [*to Mrs Bexeley*] Of course! We completely understand! Lindsay Lohan, Year Ten, here to learn how to paint skinny jeans:)

VIOLET *pinches* ISLA *on the bum.*

ISLA: [*to Mrs Bexeley*] I'm Keke Palmer, that's spelt k-e-k-e, Year Ten, and I guess I'm the skinny-jean-painting tutor.

We watch as she writes this information down on a tissue from within the depths of her bra. She's kinda old-school, and I love that.

VIOLET: I'm freaking out. Mr Glass **just** told us to get the fuck outta here and never speak to each other again—

ISLA: —Which is ridiculous—

VIOLET: —And here we are … together … in school! It's not ideal, is it?

The reality of it dawns fully on ISLA. *She does the sign of the cross while groaning 'Lord help us'.*

Silence.

VIOLET: [*whispers to* ISLA] I hate when you do that

ISLA: What? Do what?

VIOLET: That weird religious stuff. It's jarring as fuck

ISLA: I'm literally praying to save your ass right now, Violet, don't be dramatic!

VIOLET: Nah I hate that shit and you know it

ISLA: Are you joking? You hate this?

ISLA *does the sign of the cross again.* VIOLET *squirms.*

You're being ridiculous.

VIOLET *begins to raise her voice.*

VIOLET: No I'm not!—

The unseen Mrs Bexeley looks up at this.

ISLA: [*as Mrs Bexeley*] 'Everything okay?'

ISLA *pulls a face at* VIOLET *as if to shush her.* VIOLET *stays in a state of discomfort.*

Yeah sorry, Miss, we're all good.

[*As Mrs Bexeley*] 'Good. Fifteen minutes till the building closes. Have a good weekend—er—Lindsay and Keke.'

And with that, she's gone. [*Silly voice*] Thank fuck!

VIOLET *is seething. She can't even look at* ISLA. *Of course, this only makes* ISLA *want to provoke her.*

Violet.

Violet.

Violeeeeet.

ISLA *gets nothing in return. She decides to feign possession; an attempt to annoy her friend into submission. Her eyes roll backwards and she convulses as if The Power Of Christ is truly Within Her.* VIOLET *is horrified.*

VIOLET: stop, Isla—

ISLA *continues. She whispers the words 'Our Father Who Art In Heaven, Hallow'd Be Thy Name'.*

ISLA, MAN! I SAID STOP DOING THAT SHIT!—

ISLA *continues.* VIOLET *grabs* ISLA *by the shoulders, hard. It's the most imposing she's been.*

FUCK STOP ALRIGHT? What's wrong with you? Seriously? Something's severely fucking wrong with you to find so much enjoyment out of pissing me the fuck off. This is so classic you. Doing something that clearly makes me uncomfortable and you push and you push and you keep fucking pushing and taking all the air out of the room till you get a reaction outta me and—

ISLA: Omg I was just having a laugh—

VIOLET: Oh fuck off, okay? Don't act like you didn't just hear me say stop.

She vocally expresses rage.

See? You get me to this place, man. I—Ugh! You want the real tea, Isla? If you're so big and bad—

ISLA: Aiight I'm ready, go on den big man—

VIOLET: I'm not a man!—

ISLA: Violet it's a phrase oh my god relax—

VIOLET: [*to the audience*] Annnnd now she'll act innocent—

ISLA: —Violet, stop tryna win them over, man, you're actually pissing me off—

VIOLET: —STOP CALLING ME A MAN THEN, ISLA! Fuck! You know what, I let you have your piss-weak, Kamala Harris election speech about your absent 'father', but do you know what's interesting? Here's the tea for you, Isla.

ISLA: I swear down if you say what I think you're about to say—

VIOLET: You sit there and you say you're soooo different to him, that you could never be him, but in actuality …

one: you both called me a man
two: you both can't own up to your shit and
three: you both hurt the closest people in your lives!

One minute you're smart, unstoppable, fuck the world, next minute you're telling me I'm crazy and have a 'boy bod'. You don't listen to me when I say 'stop', or 'please don't do that fucking religious impression' or even today! Following me here—

ISLA: You're the one who came in here—

VIOLET: But you knew I'd come here—

ISLA: How could I know that?—

VIOLET: You know fucking everything about me and that's not healthy, Isla! You're not my boyfriend—

ISLA: —Thank God—

VIOLET: —And I got a lot going on rn so I'm out of energy for you acting like you love and care about me, when you do these things that just takes us right back to stage one! The whiplash of it all is so jarring!

ISLA: Okay what are you even talking about right now?

VIOLET: I'm talking about this

She mocks the sign of the cross.

bullshit you been doing!

ISLA: I'm not even Christian myself and you know that.

VIOLET: It's violent as fuck and represents all of the violence that's happening in the world right now.

ISLA: [*like a cowgirl*] whoa nelly! whooa nelly!

VIOLET: Nah I'm sick of it! Look, I'll make it reeeeeeal simple for you. Does your mum go to Church, yes or no?

ISLA: yea

VIOLET: Does your dad go to Church, yes or no?

ISLA: I don't know what he does—

VIOLET: YES OR NO

ISLA: yes. he did.

VIOLET: am I your best friend, yes or no?

ISLA: yes. obviously.

VIOLET: This is it! This is the problem! This is where it alllll started. When you and your mum thought it would be a good idea to invite me to Easter. That was …

A sudden, abrupt blackout. Even VIOLET *didn't see this coming. It's scary. This is the first dark dissociation that we have seen so far. A cube of light appears at the side of the stage. Relentless sounds of a ball bouncing.*

I—what the fuck? Isla?

Beat.

I—what? I—

She tries to find a joke within it all but fails clumsily.

This isn't real, this isn't real, Violet, this isn't real.

She waits for it to be over. The ball bounces faster.

This is so fucked. Can you guys see that? It's like a small, pressurised box with like … this … fuck! Ugh! This fucking ball just bouncing, bouncing, bouncing on every side.

She retches. Apologises to the audience.

Are you guys still there? Hello? I'm not being funny. Can someone just say something?

At last, she hears ISLA*'s voice again, overlapping with the bouncing—*

ISLA: Violet! Violet! VIOLET!

VIOLET: Isla?

The sound subsides. Lights back up on stage. Everything is exactly the same as before. Only VIOLET *is rattled by this.*

ISLA: Where the fuck did you go?

VIOLET: What?

ISLA: You were geeing up to victimise yourself about some antics at Easter and then you go all weird on me.

VIOLET: I—no that's not—I—you didn't just go with me? To that place?

ISLA: What place? What the fuck? WHAT HAPPENED AT EASTER, VIOLET? Do I have to prise it outta you? I mean when did this even happen?

VIOLET: Uh, a year ago, almost?

VIOLET *tries to regain normalcy. She paces and avoids eye contact with* ISLA.

And I ain't never felt the same with your family since. I didn't have the capacity to stand up for myself let alone do it in a fucking place of worship! What did you think would happen? All of the evidence in the world shows you what the Church thinks and feels about gays let alone trans people. Think about the history! You really thought it would be a cute bonding experience? Another reminder that there's a whoooleee like … industry that hates me. That wants to change me. 'Cleanse' me or whatever.

And my best friend, my sister, fucking supports it. Believes in it. I can't even—

ISLA: I don't support it necess—

VIOLET: What's this then?

She mocks the sign of the cross.

Silence.

ISLA: My peoples never chose to be Christian, it wasn't like a box on a form that we ticked to say: yuppp that's a bit of me, I think I'll go with this one. No. It was you lot who came on your fucking boats with your disease and your grand idea of colonising half of the fucking world—

VIOLET: —

ISLA: You're literally Dutch, like you're thee OG colonisers of the West Indies, like I don't know what to tell you. You ain't about to admit it? I hear you, cuz it's fucking awful. But it's yours, babe. Not mine. Not my guilt, or my family's guilt. That's for y'all to deal with.

VIOLET: —and I am dealing with that.

ISLA: So you ain't about to sit there and judge me or my family or any of them other black people you met that Easter at Church, alright?

Silence.

VIOLET: You don't know what they done to me there. You don't know what they said.

ISLA: [*dismisses*] Oh god here we go—

VIOLET: Can I just?

Inhale.

it was in the looks, okay? The shakes of their heads, the laughter. That's a classic; the fucking laughter. Me, just being me, was the funniest thing in the world. And then there's that guy—

ISLA: Oh my god it was a whole year ago what guy are you even talking about?

VIOLET: I don't know who he is but he's fully grown. Like a man. He came up behind me and whispered in my ear …

Shudders.

ew I feel gross even thinking about it—

ISLA: What'd he say?

VIOLET *begins staring offstage in the direction of the bouncing ball. The lighting starts to go dark around her again.*

VIOLET: Oh my god, not this again … it's not real, it's not real, it's not real—

ISLA: VIOLET! Don't start this shit again!

VIOLET *is jolted back into reality.*

What'd he say?

VIOLET: 'You're an abomination.' Is what he said. And he laughed.

He did, Isla. I didn't even know what that word meant, really. I knew it was bad, obvi, but I had to go home and look it up to fully deep what he was saying. Like what is that? Being too young to understand the insults that people are dishing you, for just existing?

The rest of that fucking day I was outta my body, checked out, you know? And I told myself after that … I told myself real friends wouldn't put me through that. And I still agree with that statement.

Silence.

ISLA: But I didn't know he said that, Violet. I didn't know.

VIOLET: Sure, you didn't know about that one guy … but don't act like you didn't know that Church was a bad idea?

ISLA: It was a big deal for me to invite a friend into that part of my life. That shit is sacred to me, yeah? My people having hope in something. Having community. A place to go to where we sing and show love and talk about actualising our dreams. That shit is sacred to me, Violet, and I swear down, I was just tryna share all that with you.

VIOLET: It's sacred to YOU, Isla. It's scary for me. And … look I can't lie, Isla, respectfully, sometimes the worst shit I get is from black people. Caribbean people.

Long, painful silence.

A spotlight surrounds only ISLA.

ISLA: Guys I don't know what to do, I can hear Violet still talking but it's all muffled because my fucking brain feels like it's firing really fast and my heart, i can feel it coming out my chest and I dunno I just—I just keep seeing all the imaginations that I made in my head, the ones that made me feel so happy and safe, I feel like they're all disappearing. I've made all these little scenes in my mind over the years, like seeing Violet walk in her first fashion week in Milan and how proud of her I'd be when I turn to Rihanna and say 'yeah that's my sister' or—or me being in labour and pushing a whole ass human out of me and Violet being there telling me not to be a 'pussyhole' and that I can do anything and to pUuuUUushhHHhhh and I thought about what we would be like when we're old, like really old—

She says 'no shade' to an older person in the audience.

—how nice it would feel to have her by my side at the end part of my life, how much fun we'd still have in the nursing home and—and—and the pranks we'd pull on the other residents, like, like swapping our wigs or racing our zimmerframes or something

She laughs through her tears.

and how we'd still kind of be having sleepovers in our own way, just with adult nappies and prescription drugs. And i just, i can't stop seeing all those images disappearing, and i don't want that to happen cuz cuz cuz I wanted to do my whole life with her and—and—and I'm panicking but I'm tryna listen to her, to what she's saying and—and—

The spotlight fades away and we're back to reality, where VIOLET *overlaps in with:*

VIOLET: They been calling me a batty boy and laughing at me on buses or trains or when I'm walking home, since day one. They've been doing gun signs and talking about going to hell when they're around me. Shaking their heads. All of it. You've seen it yourself.

ISLA: yeah and every time I say something

VIOLET: and then you Kiki with them two days later!

ISLA: THEY'RE MY COMMUNITY, VIOLET! Whatdya want me to do?

VIOLET: —it only gets worse when I'm with your uncles or at Carnival or

ISLA: but—but—but at carnival my aunties fed you after everything went down! remember? they gave you ackee and saltfish and you got the *most* plantains i've ever fucking *seen* and uncle goldie waited for you so he could drive you home, and **YES** i know he said some crazy things that day and i **know** that's not good enough but that's how they show up!!! they make sure you're fed and safe and—

VIOLET: —it's even worse at Church. I can't be putting myself in that position no more.

ISLA: Fuck! Fine I won't invite you to church again!

Beat. VIOLET *fidgets uncomfortably.* ISLA *slowly reads between the lines.*

Please don't tell me you're on some other ting.

?

VIOLET: I dunno, Isla. Like Mr Glass said, maybe we're not good … or enough for each other. Maybe we needed this … *us* … for an era in our lives? And maybe that era's passed?

ISLA: Stop. Nah stop, V, I can't hear it—

VIOLET: You gotta listen sometimes. You've got your own people. I've seen you—

ISLA: —No you're not hearing me, I can't—I gotta gay—go! I gotta go!

ISLA *makes her way to the door. It's like she physically can't cope with what* VIOLET *is saying.*

VIOLET *blocks her.*

VIOLET: —you've been hanging out at the Ritzy with some of the Faulkner girls, and on the courts with the boys. And you seem happy, laughing and that, I've seen you! And I, did you hear about this? I got into—

BOTH: [*at the same time*] —Heaven with a fake ID—

ISLA: Yeah. I know. It was plastered all over Instagram.

VIOLET: Come on, Isla! You can never just be happy for me! I—I've finally found people who can just be excited about my wins!

ISLA: Who, what? Just blindly agree with you?—

ISLA *is still dodging* VIOLET *in an attempt to leave.*

MOVE, VIOLET!

VIOLET *blocks her.*

[*Exasperated*] I—ugh! Why can't you just let me leave?

VIOLET: I will. I just need you to hear me, like to really fucking hear what I'm tryna say to you, okay?

Beat.

I'm really good right now, Isla. I'm healthy. I'm almost done with school. have a friendship group. The only thing that's messy in my life right now, is you. Full shade. There has to come a point when I look around and really deep what the common denominator is in all of this … and I just … I'm tired, you know? And I'm suspended right now, which is really shit, and also because of you. I can't keep going like this and I can't repeat next year cause my mum won't get child support any more so I need to work … I don't even know why I'm justifying myself so much! Look, I have to break the pattern, okay?

Beat.

ISLA: And—just to be clear—**I'm** the 'pattern'?

Awkward silence as ISLA *crumples into the armchair.*

VIOLET: Wellllllll if the shoe fits?

Beat. ISLA *is crushed. This is so painful.*

ISLA: Fuck you.

VIOLET: You can go now.

VIOLET *steps away from the door. There's momentary stillness between the two girls before* ISLA *remarks:*

ISLA: That has to be the most 'Violet' thing to do

VIOLET: What?

ISLA: Look me dead in the eyes, tell me to get out and lie to me about everything being fine.

VIOLET: I'm not lying.

ISLA: [*sarcastically*] Violet, I beg you give me at least a smidge of respect right now

VIOLET: I don't know what you're fucking talking about

ISLA *walks defiantly to the supply cupboard. She pulls out a big duffel sports bag, with* VIOLET*'s initials V.E. printed on it.*

ISLA: What's this then?

Silence.

VIOLET: [*in a small voice*] that's my PE bag

They both look at the bag.

ISLA: What was that thing you were saying? About everything being fine?

Silence.

Look at me.

VIOLET *turns to face* ISLA.

Why are you sleeping at school?

Long, long silence.

Tell me

VIOLET: how'd you know?

ISLA: of course I know

ISLA *unzips the bag on the table.* VIOLET *looks away as she pulls out pairs of underwear, pyjamas, a hair-dryer, a brush, headphones, another pair of shoes, tablets, a toiletry bag.*

Beat.

How'd you not get caught?

Beat.

Hmm?

VIOLET: Well … I did …

ISLA: what?

VIOLET: Mr Glass caught me …

Silence. ISLA *tries to make sense of all of this.*

ISLA: I don't get it.

VIOLET: On Tuesdays and Thursdays the cleaners come. And on Fridays the Headmaster locks each room before he closes the building.

ISLA *looks around for her phone to check the time.*

We got ten minutes, Isla, you really gotta get outta here I can't express it enough—

Almost exactly as she says this, the door rattles. Silence. It rattles again, this time more aggressive. The girls mouth to each other 'who is it?' 'well I don't fucking know do I?' as the door keeps rattling, knocking, rattling some more.

The freakish voice of Mr Glass rings out:

MR GLASS: [*voiceover*] 'Violet? Are you in there? Why is the door locked?'

We hear the sound of keys jangling. The girls ***panic supreme!!! This is like so so so beyond bad.*** *The following lines between the girls are more whispered + mouthed than anything.*

VIOLET: FUCK FUCK FUCK FUCK
ISLA: hide in the closet!!!! Omg HIDE IN THE CLOSET!!!
VIOLET: Are you mad? I just fucking got outta the closet ain't no way

Dreamgirls*' 'no way no no no way' begins but it's like the worst time possible to do this bit.*

NO! I'm not going back in there
MR GLASS: [*voiceover*] 'You're really going to make me use the janitor's keys? How disappointing.'

ISLA, *in a flurry of chaotic movement, hides desperately in the cupboard.* VIOLET *runs to meet the unseen Mr Glass at the door. If he was disgusting in Scene One, he's now HORRIFIC.*

SCENE SEVEN

MR GLASS: [*voiceover*] 'I knew you were foolish but this takes the biscuit. Are you trying to embarrass me?'
VIOLET: No Sir, of course not.
MR GLASS: [*voiceover*] 'What did we **just** talk about?'

Beat. VIOLET *is small and vulnerable.*

VIOLET: [*meekly*] That I have to pack my things.

Beat.

MR GLASS: [*voiceover*] 'And???'

He waits for her to continue.

VIOLET: and leave?

MR GLASS: [*voiceover*] 'So your ears do work. Funny that.'

VIOLET *begins to panic.*

VIOLET: I—I … I don't know where I'm meant to go.

He begins to roar at her. It's awful and mean and degrading. As he does so, VIOLET *moves around the space quickly. She repacks her bag.*

MR GLASS: [*voiceover*] 'Newsflash! **I DON'T CARE.** You can sleep on a park bench or a street corner for all it's worth! And guess what? **IT'S NOT WORTH ANYTHING.** My reputation is on the line by a little—er— [*Scoffing*] **child** who can't abide by a simple rule! ENOUGH. I gave you the opportunity to sleep here last week and all I wanted in return was separation from that mouthy brat that you go around with but today is where I draw the line.
GET. OUT. And Lord knows, we don't need you to come back.'

VIOLET: okay. I just need to change out of my uniform, Sir, if you wouldn't mind.

Mr Glass bumbles incoherently a series of 'ums' and 'erms' and 'harrumphs' and 'I'm locking this room in eight minutes and you better be gone' as he awkwardly exits the room. Loser.

SCENE EIGHT

Lighting shift. ISLA *peels out of the cupboard in pure shock. Perhaps there's a gay gag about coming out of the closet?*

ISLA: That's fucked.
That is so so fucked.

VIOLET: I don't have the energy for your political campaign, Isla.
That was the most fucked-up situation.

ISLA: Yup.

ISLA *plays a few seconds of Mr Glass's vitriol that she obviously just recorded on her phone. She's interrupted by* VIOLET *repeating 'fuck' which makes her turn the recording off.*

Well, I didn't know what to do.

Beat.

VIOLET *shrinks into a smaller, more vulnerable version of herself. She holds her head in her hands.*

VIOLET: Fuck. Fuck, fuck, FUCK!

I didn't want it to go like that. You have to believe me. I just wanted to come up here, get my shit, ugly cry on the roof with a cigarette and leave. I didn't want to see you. I didn't wanna fight.

She groans.

You're so … like … embedded in everything. It all runs so deep and sometimes I don't wanna be held accountable or looked at knowingly or reminded of some mistake I made when I was a kid. I want to be met as the new version of me.

Why haven't you interrupted me yet?

ISLA: Don't have anything to add.

VIOLET: Hmmm.

Can you sit beside me at least?

ISLA: Aren't you annoyed at me?

VIOLET: Yes. I am. But can u just come here so I can articulate myself?

ISLA *sighs and enters from the vom and positions herself perched on a chair beside* VIOLET.

With you it's too messy because we feel so much for each other that I kind of forget that I'm not you. That in fact there are huge wastelands of understanding between us.

Like on paper, you know more about me than I do. But when it comes to how it **feels** to be me? You're lost, man. I figured out I was trans before I even knew what it meant. And I still haven't found the words that feel 'right' in describing how it feels, at its core. It's—It's like …

She genuinely struggles to describe it.

You grew up surrounded by community. Me? I'd never even seen a happy trans person til like two years ago. How crazy is that?

I found my community through the internet. Meanwhile, everyone says I'm addicted to it. You tell me all the time. That I shouldn't pick up my phone the second I hear a notification. That I should diversify what I consume. And I hear that.

But what you don't get is: it's really hard to separate yourself from the thing that introduced you to yourself. What I've made on my phone is this whole algorithm of content that connects me to the other people in the sea with me. I've got them all squished into this endless stream of voices and conversations and reads and ballroom clips and baby goats in little costumes and non binary baby reveals and ADHD tips and tricks and wig instals and activism and comedy sets and makeup tutorials, which make me feel, just for those moments, like I'm surrounded. Like I've built something that echoes what I'm feeling on the inside. And it feels good. And I don't wanna give that up.

But it's dangerous, you know? Because I've built this thing that knows who I am, who knows my T, so then when something really fucked up happens in real life, like an assault or a murder or a law or a bill or some TERF spurting some hate speech or nazis roaming the streets that reaffirms that the world outside of my phone still fucking hates trans people, it's sent straight to me. And then the floor is wiped from beneath me, you know? That feeling, that moment of safety? gone. And then I cry for a bit. But not long enough, there could never be long enough.

But somehow, I come back to the undeniable fact that being trans feels like the most natural thing in the world. There's nothing I need to 'learn', it just is. And whether people believe it or not doesn't really matter because I know what I know.

Pause.

SCENE NINE

ISLA: I believe it, Violet.

ISLA *sits beside* VIOLET.

VIOLET: I know. You always did. I think subconsciously I felt like I owed you for that.

ISLA: Really?

VIOLET: yeah.

ISLA: you know that weird feeling when someone names the exact experience you've been having? It's like déjà vu but …

VIOLET *shrugs.*

I always felt like I owed you for saving me at Karim's fourteenth birthday.

VIOLET: oh my god I haven't thought about that for years

ISLA: Really? I think about it all the time.

I remember it was at Karim's house, and my older brother, TJ, was friends with his older brother—

VIOLET: you ain't gotta say his name.

ISLA *smirks.*

ISLA: We were all in the garden by the grill and I heard all the older boys suddenly start laughing, like something really funny had happened maybe, and so I looked up, just casually, and I don't wanna sound crazy but so many of them were looking at me.

Felt like they'd been watching me for ages. You know when you just feel like prey? In a split second you've gone from whatever menial thought you were having to being so aware of all these people just watching you.

She looks out at the audience who are in fact watching her.

Every time that happens … that look … like they've been willing you to meet their gaze, when you finally do, they just seem so chuffed with themselves. As if it's the first and last time you'll ever experience that. As if one day i'll sit down with my grandkids and say 'ahhh yes a man looked at me once'. It's so corny.

And you know what's so embarrassing? I liked it. When I saw them all smiling and leering and dapping each other up, I felt important. I felt special. Like I had succeeded at womanhood. I swear down; it was my first big: oooohhh 'misogyny feels good' moment. And maybe I revelled in that feeling too much and I let them see that I enjoyed it cuz I remember Karim's brother yelled something like 'come get it if you want it, darlin.'

And then I just … plummeted. The aftertaste was so *sour.* I felt disgusting. Like I'd bathed in mud. Like maggots were feeding on my skin. Like—do you wanna know the real tea? I felt like a pervert. For real, I felt **that** guilty.

Everyone was beckoned inside in time to sing 'Happy Birthday', and so the lights were off because candles? Cake? You get it.

Everyone's focus is on Karim and singing so nobody notices his brother put his tongue on my neck and both his hands on my boobs, positioning himself and his boner on the bottom of my spine.

I couldn't believe what was happening. And, so publically? I—I couldn't wrap my head around it. It was really scary, bestie. and I kept looking for you or TJ but I couldn't—i—I couldn't even move. I felt so small and dumb, and all I remember telling myself is 'you like it, you like it, you like it, you like it, you like it, you're supposed to, you like it'

Later, when the lights were back on and people spilled back into the garden, I tried to act really normal and I thought I was doing a good job until you came up to me and asked why my face was grey. You said you'd never seen me look like that. Not even when I had gastro.

I can't remember how we got from there to the bathroom but I bet you just dragged me by the hand, knowing that I needed something—not sure what—but something. D'ya remember how much I vomited? I've never been sick from a feeling before. You had smacked one hand across my forehead, holding my edges down so that they didn't sweat off and make me feel worse than I already did. I told you I loved you so much.

Beat. She reflects. The lighting goes kind of dissociative, kind of reality. A middle ground.

When I was done yakking my guts down the toilet bowl, you wiped my face and told me that you had a method for when things like this happen.

They turn in to face one another. Holding hands. Eyes firmly shut. Cutesy.

VIOLET: 'Think about what it smelled like after school at Mrs Kumar's house.'

ISLA: What?

VIOLET: 'Think about it'

'Focus on the smell of her incense, the hints of ghee cooking on the stove, the smell of home-made sweets on a platter. Think about how there was never any overhead lighting; it was always candlelit and orange-tinted lamps. And if you focus hard enough you might be able to hear'—

ISLA: *Coronation Street* playing on the telly!!!

VIOLET: 'Exactly! When they look at you like that and you don't think you can do anything to stop it, or call them out, and nobody will believe you because they're married or respected or whatever, you have to make your mind take you somewhere else. It helps, I promise.'

The lighting slowly returns to reality across ISLA*'s next few lines.*

ISLA: Oh my days, I don't think I've ever felt sadder than that night. When I got home I felt really, really … empty. I wondered how many times you'd experienced that feeling? I tried to picture your face all grey like you said mine was and I felt so shit, bestie. And I told myself that I owe you every bit of loyalty and love that I got in me cuz it was so unfair that you had to go through that alone in order to save me.

VIOLET: Do you know what's funny?

Pause.

We just spent a really long time in reality. We didn't do the whole leaving-our-bodies-and-making-a-game thing.

The girls look around the space and the audience.

How do you feel?

ISLA: I feel fine.

They both audibly gasp.

VIOLET: Me too. Maybe we don't need it all the time.

ISLA: Tea. Like it's just an option for survival, not the only thing—

She is interrupted by the final school closure notice.

SCENE TEN

VOICEOVER: This is a closure notice. The whole school building will close in five minutes. Thank you.

VIOLET: fuck fuck fuck

VIOLET *scoops her upturned items back into her PE bag.*

ISLA: Whatta you doing?

VIOLET: I dunno, Isla, **something**. What can I do? I can't go home and I can't stay here cuz obviously the suspension changes things—

ISLA *starts helping to pack her things.*

ISLA: I actually hate him so much it's not funny. Why didn't you tell me earlier?

VIOLET: Cuz I wanted you to leave so I could figure my own shit out! I didn't wanna rely on you any more!

ISLA: Violet, you're my sister. You gotta rely on me. Forever, okay? Forever. This is so fucking corny but for real; I'm not leaving if you're not leaving and I'm not safe if you're not safe. So just, shut up! Okay?

The girls begin to cry and laugh at themselves while they do so. The love is soooo undeniably real.

Also—I feel so embarrassed that I let you down that Easter and many times since that. I'm really sorry. But tonight you're staying at mine and it'll be just me, you and my mum. Nobody else. I promise.

VIOLET: okay.

ISLA: And … look … I got a community who can speak about something that's not right. And so do you. One thing about black people? Yappa yappa yappa. One thing about gays? Fucking yappa yappa yappa. And I'm sorry, but that guy's a fucking loser and I'm tryna tear him a new asshole. So just … let me just do my damn ting.

ISLA *cracks her neck, then starts typing furiously on her phone. She paces as she does so.* VIOLET *finishes packing everything up. On the screen behind them,* ISLA*'s words are shown. She writes:*

'BEAST OF A HEADTEACHER @ ST JOHNS, FORMER 'ROYAL PUBLIC SCHOOL AWARD WINNER' COMMITS NEGLIGENCE, HATE CRIME AND OVERALL GROTESQUENESS BY KICKING OUT A YOUNG TRANS GIRL MODEL'

ISLA *goes 'hmm?' and flashes her phone at* VIOLET, *who, replies in a satisfying 'mmm'.*

(HEADSHOT ATTACHED PURRRR)

Her fab headshot flashes on the screen.

'EXPERIENCING HOMELESSNESS.
NAME = MR MICHAEL GLASS.
GET HIM, DIVAS'

We see ISLA *attach an audio file on this post.*

The 'post' sound effect rings out.

I posted it on everything. Threads, Twitter, Facebook, even Tumblr so the Ethel Cain stans can talk their talk.

VIOLET *checks her phone and reposts on all platforms.*

VIOLET: Imma repost but fuck Elon Musk.
ISLA: Period. And fuck Zuckerberg too.

Beat.

VIOLET: I love you so much.
ISLA: I love you too.

The girls head for the door. They start leaving as they speak the next few lines:

Got everything?
VIOLET: Mmm. Can we get Wingstop?
ISLA: Yesss bitch, of course.

With only their heads peeking out, they remember the audience.

Oh! It was so fab ki'ing with y'all <3
VIOLET: See you later divas!
ISLA: Stay fabulous!

VIOLET *finds the aunty or uncle she clocked at the beginning.*

VIOLET: Respect, Aunty!

And with one in-sync 'Biiiig Uppppp', the girls leave.

SCENE ELEVEN / EPILOGUE

The school bell rings. An announcement says:

VOICEOVER: This is a closure notice. All rooms will be locked and the building closed for the weekend.

A flurry of phone-notification sounds. The screen shows all the reactions and responses the girls get from their audiences. There are ***SO*** *many people cussing Mr Glass out. Some look like this:*

JEMIMA ALLEN—Age 64, Kingstown Jamaica—'Dis man should go suck his mudda before he come corrupt the yutes like this.'

ANDI NEWFARM—Age 52, London, United Kingdom—'Hello munchkin. This is terrible. He sounds like a real shithead. I have shared with everyone I know. Full support.'

KALESHA MOTTLEY—Age 16, London, United Kingdom—'errrrgggghhhh he so nasty for this! Big up my cousin for speaking up!'

CAZ FRANCIS—Age 70, Hobart, Tasmania—'Dirty little fucker'

LYNN HARRIES—Age 26, London, United Kingdom—'Oh bestie, this man is raggedy hip! 25 to life I say!'

CHANDICE BAXTER—Age 31, Bridgetown, Barbados—'Nasty rassclaart man! Karma gon get him'

DENISE DIREEN—Age 68, Berkshire, United Kingdom—'Tell this sweet girl that my pantry is filled and my spare room is empty if she needs a safe place. I can pop the electric blanket on at any moment!'

BIMINI BOM BOULASH—Age X, London, United Kingdom—'It's always some beast tryna get a diva down. As Ru said, "he should get off the cross, we could use the wood!"'

The sounds of a radio station intro are heard. 'Hello and welcome to Brixton Radio, it's your host Tony-T coming live and direct from South London! Today I'm blessed to be joined with two boss ladies from St John's Public School after they went viral online for outing their raahtid Headmaster! My stomach's splittin from laughing with these 2 yutes, they got bare bare jokes, bare vibes—I swear down these girls need a TV show! World domination! There's a gofundme link that's getting mad results so please donate if you got di funds. Imma say wagwan to Isla and Violet right after this track!'

'No Bars' by JT plays out through the curtain call. To the actors: please feel free to feel yourselves as much as you want during the bows <3

END OF PLAY

RIFFIN THEATRE COMPANY PRESENTS
GREEN DOOR THEATRE COMPANY PRODUCTION
N ASSOCIATION WITH BELVOIR ST THEATRE

SISTREN

Y IOLANTHE

APR – 3 MAY 2026
DOWNSTAIRS THEATRE, BELVOIR ST THEATRE

RIFFIN
HEATRE
OMPANY

GREEN DOOR
THEATRE
COMPANY

CAST & CREATIVES

Director Ian Michael
Production Designer Emma White
Lighting Designer Kelsey Lee
Composer & Sound Designer Daniel Herten
Video Designer TK Abioye
Dramaturg Dylan Van Den Berg
Voice & Accent Coach Angela Sullen
Production Managers Frankie Clarke, Tyler Fitzpatrick
Stage Manager Jen Jackson
Community Engagement Strategists Janet Anderson, Iolanthe
Directorial Attachment Zarif
Associate Production Designer Geita Goarin
With Janet Anderson, Iolanthe

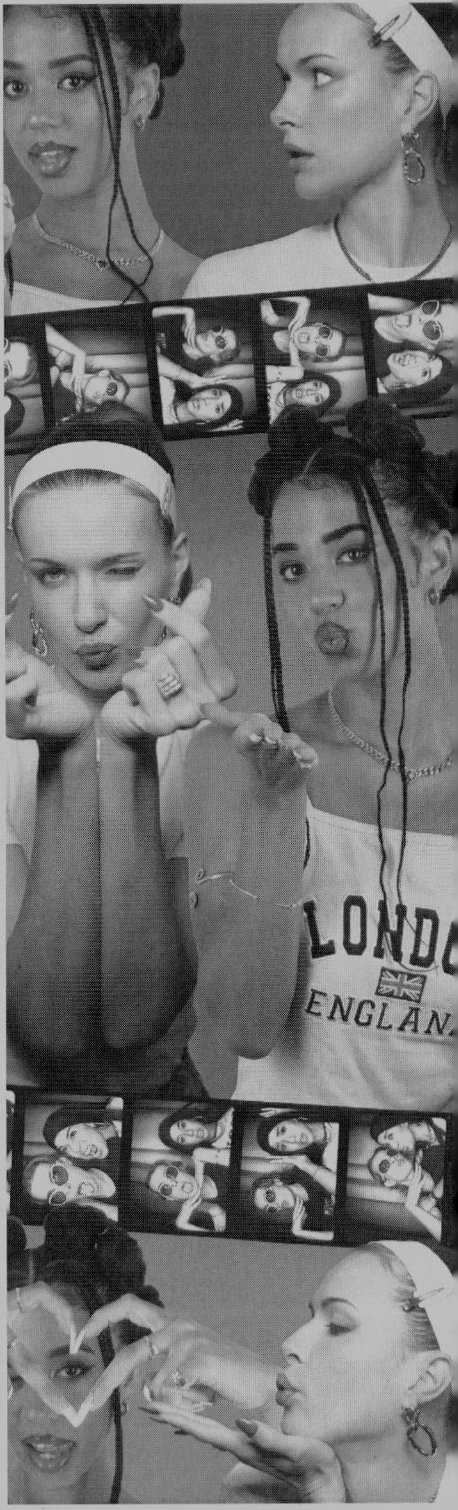

SUPPORTED BY

GOVERNMENT PARTNERS

SISTREN was supported by Australian Plays Transform through the Untold Stories Program and the premiere season was a part of Griffin Lookout 2025, supported by Shane & Cathryn Brennan. This presentation is supported by the Girgensohn Foundation.

DIRECTOR'S NOTE

SISTREN exists because these girls exist. Black girls. Trans girls. They don't just occupy space—they grab it, flip it and reverse it, and claim it. They make you laugh, make you flinch, tug at your heart and pull you into a world bigger than any of us. That refusal to be small is what powers this story and why it demands to be told.

At the heart of it? The lethal combination—Isla and Violet. Their friendship is wild and tender all at once. It's personal but political too, a statement that joy, love and identity aren't optional—they're essential. Watching them, you see them push each other, call each other out and insist on being unapologetically themselves, even when the world tries to shrink them. The sisterhood is unpredictable and unstoppable. Being themselves isn't passive—it's hilarious, rebellious and present.

And the world that **Iolanthe** has poured out onto the page moves as fast as they do. Their brains and imaginations leap between reality, memory, pop culture and fantasy. It's electric. Maybe uncomfortable. It's alive in all its chaos and silliness.

SISTREN captures the thrill of being fully yourself in a world that often refuses to make space for you. The audience is asked to lean in, to ride the chaos and still crack up along the way. What's on stage isn't just performance—it's lived experience, absolute imagination and defiance.

It's about claiming space. About refusing to make yourself smaller for anyone else. About joy that won't be erased, love that can't be contained, and life lived loud, untamed and relentless. It's a celebration of existing on your own terms—for yourself, for community and for your sistrens.

To **Iolanthe** and **Janet Anderson**—you are the heart of this. Making *SISTREN* with you is a dream. The trust, the risk, the way you show up for each other and the work carries the same wild, tender, unapologetic energy that lives inside Isla and Violet. You bring them to life with so much joy and care. Thank you, always.

To **Emma White**, **Kelsey Lee**, **Daniel Herten**, **TK Abioye**, **Dylan Van Den Berg**, **Angela Sullen**, **Jen Jackson** and **Cris Chavez**—you didn't just create this, you made it bigger and bolder. You met the world of this story head-on and pushed it further than any of us ever imagined. Thank you for seeing it and for running at it.

To our producers, **Leila Enright**, **Bernadette Fam** and **Janine Lau**—thank you for your care and belief throughout. And to Green Door Theatre Company and Griffin Theatre Company, thank you for your support and for championing this work.

Ian Michael
Director

BIOGRAPHIES

IOLANTHE

PLAYWRIGHT / COMMUNITY ENGAGEMENT STRATEGIST / ISLA

Afro-Caribbean / Australian artist Iolanthe is an actor, writer, model and self-proclaimed socialite. Spending almost all of her childhood living in England, with a Norwegian-German parent, Iolanthe's artistry is impacted by understanding the mixing of cultures and creative landscapes. In both her life and work, she tends to examine her role in society, refining the purpose of her creative talent into plays, performances, creative direction, styling, essays.

Iolanthe is a NIDA graduate (BFA Acting 2022), leaving her class with the annual Lesley Walford AM Award of excellence, taking her to study method acting at the Lee Strasberg Institute in New York.

Her theatre credits include: for Green Door Theatre Company: *SISTREN* (as part of Griffin Lookout), *seven methods of killing kylie jenner*. Iolanthe's screen work includes: for ModiBodi: *I'm Dying Inside*, for Joe Lycett: *MARK*; for Belmore Pictures Presents in association with Dark Sky Films: *Cruel Hands*; for Netflix: *Black Mirror*; for Stan Originals: *He Had It Coming*.

BIOGRAPHIES

IAN MICHAEL

DIRECTOR

Ian is a proud Noongar man and WAAPA graduate. He is a Resident Director at Sydney Theatre Company.

Ian's directing credits include, as Director: for Belvoir St Theatre: *Big Girls Don't Cry*; for Black Swan State Theatre Company and The Blue Room: *The Bleeding Tree*; for Sydney Theatre Company: *Constellations, Picnic at Hanging Rock, Stolen*; as Associate Director: for Black Swan State Theatre Company: *The Cherry Orchard*; for Black Swan State Theatre Company and Yirra Yaakin: *Skylab*; for Sydney Theatre Company: *Dracula, Strange Case of Dr Jekyll and Mr Hyde, Sweat, The 7 Stages of Grieving, The Picture of Dorian Gray, The President, The Seagull*.

As an actor, Ian has performed with companies including Sydney Theatre Company, Griffin Theatre Company, Black Swan State Theatre Company, Malthouse Theatre, Melbourne Theatre Company and ILBIJERRI Theatre Company. His writing credits include *York* (with Chris Isaacs), *HART* (with Seanna van Helten), and *Another Day in the Colony*.

He has received numerous awards and nominations, including multiple Sydney Theatre Award nominations for *Constellations* and *Stolen* and PAWA and Blue Room Awards for *The Bleeding Tree*, along with recognition from CHASS, Green Room Awards, and Fringe Festivals.

BIOGRAPHIES

EMMA WHITE

PRODUCTION DESIGNER

Emma White is a set and costume designer for stage and screen. Emma is a graduate of NIDA's Master of Fine Art Design course and has a Bachelor of Fine Art in Sculpture from UNSW Art and Design. In 2019, Emma was nominated for an APDG Award for Best Emerging Designer.

Her credits include: as Set Designer: for Sydney Theatre Company: *Oil* ; for ATYP: *The Deb*; for Hayes Theatre Co: *Godspell*; for Red Line Productions: *A Streetcar Named Desire*; as Costume Designer: for Sydney Theatre Company: *Lifespan of a Fact*; for Red Line Productions: *Seven Deadly Sins + Mahagonny Songspiel*; for NIDA: *Venus in Fur*; as Set & Costume Designer: for Griffin Theatre Company: *A is for Apple, Green Park*; for Queensland Theatre: *As You Like It*; for Squabbalogic: *The Dismissal*, for Red Line Productions: *Hand to God, Chorus*; for Belvoir 25A: *Kasama Kita*; for Campbelltown Arts Centre: *Bad Machine;* for Bondi Feast: *The Knife*; for Blue Room Theatre and Sotto: *You've Got Mail*; for Milk Crate Theatre: *Natural Order*; for National Theatre of Parramatta & Sydney Festival: *Boom*; for NIDA: *Stay Happy Keep Smiling*; for Old 505: *Homesick*; for Old 505 and Sotto: *Safe*; for Q Theatre: *Daisy Moon Was Born This Way*.

Associate Designer credits include: as Associate Costume Designer: for Sydney Theatre Company: *On the Beach*; as Associate Designer: for Hayes Theatre Co: *American Psycho*; for Sport for Jove: *A Midsummer Night's Dream, The Tempest*; as Assistant Designer: for National Theatre London: *Nine Night*; for Shakespeare's Globe: *Richard II*; for Sydney Theatre Company: *Appropriate, Lord of the Flies*.

For screen, Emma was production designer on the feature documentary *Step Into Paradise* for Blackfella Films, the television pilot *Gym Rat* for Guesswork TV, Taylor Ferguson's award-winning short film *Tough* and short film *Beautiful They*. She was costume design assistant for *PM's Daughter* (ABC) and *Mr Inbetween* S3 (Foxtel) and set designer for Shannon Murphy's short film Fractal with *AJE*. Emma has worked as production designer and costume designer on numerous TVCs.

BIOGRAPHIES

KELSEY LEE

LIGHTING DESIGNER

Kelsey's credits as Lighting Designer include: for Griffin Theatre Company: *Sex Magick, The Lewis Trilogy, Whitefella Yella Tree*; for Sydney Theatre Company: *4000 Miles*; for ATYP: *April Aardvark*; for Australian Chamber Orchestra: *There's a Sea in My Bedroom, Wilfred Gordon McDonald Partridge*; for Belvoir 25A: *An Ox Stand on My Tongue, Destroy, She Said*; for Belvoir St Theatre: *A Room of One's Own, At What Cost?, Big Girls Don't Cry, Curious Incident of the Dog in the Night-Time, Well-Behaved Women*; for Bell Shakespeare: *The Comedy of Errors*; for Blue Film: *Long Story Short*; for Ensemble Theatre: *A Letter for Molly, Killing Katie, Masterclass, Switzerland, The Memory of Water*; for Fervour: *Life Is a Dream*; for Force Majeure: *Gurr Era Op*; for Green Door Theatre Company: *Good Dog, If We Got Some More Cocaine I Could Show You How I Love You, SISTREN*; for Hayes Theatre Co: *Catch Me If You Can*; for Melbourne Theatre Company: *Destin*; for Marrugeku: *Cut the Sky, Mutiara*; for Michelle Guthrie Presents: *Tell Me on a Sunday*; for National Institute of Dramatic Art: *Lulu: A Modern Sex Tragedy*; for National Theatre of Parramatta: *A Practical Guide to Self Defence, Nothing, Queen Fatima*; for re:group collective: *Autotune*; for Sydney Dance Company: *Silence & Rapture, Somos*; for Tinderbox Productions: *Black Box: The Musical.*

Awards include the Sydney Theatre Award for Best Set Design for *Destroy, She Said*. Training: National Institute of Dramatic Art. Pronouns: she/her.

BIOGRAPHIES

DANIEL HERTEN

COMPOSER & SOUND DESIGNER

Daniel's theatre credits include: Griffin Theatre Company: *Flat Earthers: The Musical, Green Park, Pony, Sex Magick, The Lewis Trilogy, Wherever She Wanders, Whitefella Yella Tree*; for Belvoir St Theatre: *Furious Mattress, Grief Is the Thing With Feathers, Miss Peony, The Curious Incident of the Dog in the Night-Time*; for Bell Shakespeare: *Twelfth Night*; for Clockfire Theatre Company: *Plenty of Fish in the Sea*; for Darlinghurst Theatre Company: *Let the Right One In*; for Ensemble Theatre Company: *The Half-Life of Marie Curie*; for ERTH: *ARC, Shark Dive*; for essential workers: *Collapsible*; for Green Door Theatre Company: *SISTREN*; for Hayes Theatre Co: *Murder for Two, Ride the Cyclone, The Pirates of Penzance*; for National Theatre of Parramatta: *FADE*; for Performance Space: *Follies of God*; for Red Line Productions: *Hand to God, The Chairs*; for Rising Festival: *Set Piece*; for Sport for Jove: *A Midsummer Night's Dream*; for Sydney Festival: *William Yang: Milestone*; for Sydney Theatre Company: *Circle Mirror Transformation, Rules for Living, The Picture of Dorian Gray*; for Tinderbox Productions: *Black Box: The Musical.*

Training: National Institute of Dramatic Art.

TK ABIOYE

VIDEO DESIGNER

Adetokunbo (TK) Abioye is an up and coming video designer based in Sydney.

TK has recently worked on video-based shows including *Alice: Mother of Cinema and Seen*, as well as with the Video and Design teams on *Dracula* at Sydney Theatre Company. He has also been working and learning with the Stage and Company Management teams at *MJ the Musical*.

BIOGRAPHIES

DYLAN VAN DEN BERG

DRAMATURG

Dylan Van Den Berg is a Palawa writer and dramaturg, originally from the northeast of lutruwita/Tasmania. As a dramaturg, recent credits include: for Griffin Theatre Company: *Nucleus*; for Green Door Theatre Company: *SISTREN* (Griffin Lookout); for ILBIJERRI Theatre Company: *10 in 10 Play Festival, Nan's Place*; for Queensland Theatre: *Burning House*; for The Street Theatre: *A Better Tomorrow*. As a playwright, recent credits include: for Griffin Theatre Company/ Sydney Theatre Company/La Boite: *Whitefella Yella Tree*; for The Street Theatre: *Milk, The Chosen Vessel*; for the National Institute of Dramatic Art: *All that Glitters is Not Mould*; for Belco Arts: *Ngadjung*; for FlickFlick City/Hobart Fringe: *The Camel*. For his writing, he has received the Griffin Award, two AWGIES, the David Williamson Prize, two NSW Premier's Literary Awards and was shortlisted for the Bruntwood International Playwriting Prize. He is currently under commission with Griffin Theatre Company and Malthouse Theatre.

FRANKIE CLARKE

PRODUCTION MANAGER

Frankie Clarke is an independent artist working across Production Management and Lighting Design, with a deep respect for the theatrical form and the stories it creates pathways for. They have worked with Green Door Theatre Company to deliver two national tours: *Overflow* and *Burgerz* as part of the Trans Theatre Festival, as well as working on a myriad of design works across dance, theatre and installation.

BIOGRAPHIES

ANGELA SULLEN

VOICE & ACCENT COACH

Angela Nica Sullen is an Italian, African American actor from the United States. She grew up in California and on Noongar country in Western Australia. Angela is an Actor, Vocal Coach, Writer, MC and self-proclaimed comedian. Now based on Gadigal land, she studied at the National Institute of Dramatic Art, completing Bachelor of Fine Arts (Acting,2016) and Master in Fine Arts (Voice,2020). She was Associate Lecturer for Voice at NIDA.

Vocal and Dialect Coaching credits include: for Green Door Theatre Company and Darlinghurst Theatre Company: *seven methods of killing kylie jenner*; for Green Door Theatre Company: *Chewing Gum Dreams*; for NIDA: *God's Country, An Octoroon*; for Riverside Theatres: *Choir Boy*; for Sydney Theatre Company: *Grand Horizons, City of Gold, Hubris and Humiliation, Do Not Go Gentle*. Angela is working on *Seen* a new television series produced by Rough Diamond, inspired by *Brown Skin Girl* a play she collaborated with creative collective Black birds.

Acting credits include: for Griffin Theatre Company: *Orange Thrower*; for Australian Chamber Orchestra and Belvoir St Theatre: *Bridgetower*; for Force Majeure: *Nothing To Lose, Blackbirds*; for Red Line Productions: *A Streetcar Named Desire, Brown Skin Girl, Faust*; for Sydney Theatre Company: *Mosquitos, The House on Boundary Road, A Raisin in the Sun*. Angela's screen credits include: for Stan: *Bump, I am Woman*; for NBC: *La Brea*; for Seven Network: *Home & Away*; for Netflix: *Pieces of Her*; for ABC: *Mother & Son, Optics*; for Paramount+: *One Night, The Fall Guy.*

BIOGRAPHIES

TYLER FITZPATRICK

PRODUCTION MANAGER

As Production Manager: for Griffin Theatre Company: *Blaque Showgirls, Jailbaby, Pony*; for Milk Crate Theatre: *Dust*; for National Theatre of Parramatta: *Nothing*; for National Theatre of Parramatta and Merrigong Theatre Company: *A Practical Guide to Self Defence*; for Campbelltown Arts Centre: *The Other Side, Mirage, The Complication of Lyrebirds*; for Blush Opera: *Chop Chef*; for Shopfront Arts Co-Op: all productions from 2020-2025.

As Stage Manager: for Griffin Theatre Company: *The Lewis Trilogy*; for Griffin Theatre Company and Adelaide Festival: *Whitefella Yella Tree*; for CAAP and Sydney Festival: *The Bridal Lament*; for National Theatre of Parramatta and La Boite Theatre: *Yoga Play*; for Green Door Theatre Company: *seven methods of killing kylie jenner*; for Merrigong Theatre Company: *As Luck Would Have It, Trash Talk*; for Q Theatre: *The Ugliest Duckling*; for VoxStep: *Garden of Sound*; for Wright&Grainger: *Orpheus, Eurydice*.

As Assistant Stage Manager: for Griffin Theatre Company and Sydney Theatre Company *Whitefella Yella Tree*.

As Lighting Designer: for Purple Tape Productions: *[YOUR NAME], Party Girl, Expiration Date*; for Belvoir 25a: *Moon Rabbit Rising, Porpoise Pool, Aurat Raj*; for QTopia: *Notes on a Scandal, I Want it That Gay*; for Legit Theatre Co: *Misery Loves Company*; for Shopfront Arts Co-Op: *Death of a Junior Salesman*. As Producer: Purple Tape Productions: *werkaholics, [YOUR NAME], Fledgling, Party Girl, Expiration Date, Come Again, Maa Ki Rasoi, Tape Over Festival*.

Positions: Co-Founder Purple Tape Productions, Production and Operations Manager at Shopfront Arts Co-Op (2020-2025), Production Associate - Paperjam Partners (2021-2023)

Other: Touring Stage Manager with *Little Squirt* UK Tour 2025. Awards: 2022 Sydney Theatre Award for Best Lighting Design (Independent) *Moon Rabbit Rising*. Training: University of Wollongong. Pronouns: she/her

BIOGRAPHIES

JEN JACKSON

STAGE MANAGER

Jen Jackson is a Korean-Australian stage manager based on Gadigal land and a graduate of the National Institute of Dramatic Art, with a particular passion for new Australian work and a commitment to diversity in theatre.

As Stage Manager: Griffin Theatre Company: *Golden Blood, End Of., Koreaboo, Pony*; Contemporary Asian Australian Performance: *Double Delicious, The Bridal Lament, Lost in Shanghai*; Belvoir St Theatre: *A Mirror, Lose to Win*; Ensemble Theatre: *Master Class*; National Theatre of Parramatta: *Nothing*. As Assistant Stage Manager: Belvoir St Theatre: *At What Cost, Song of First Desire*; Pinchgut Opera: *Rinaldo.*

JANET ANDERSON

COMMUNITY ENGAGEMENT STRATEGIST / VIOLET

Janet Anderson graduated from the National Institute of Dramatic Arts in 2022, having previously studied at Newtown High School of Performing Arts.

Janet's theatre credits include: for Belvoir St Theatre: *Orlando*; for essential workers: *Collapsible*; for Green Door Theatre Company: *SISTREN* (as part of Griffin Lookout); for Green Door Theatre Company and Darlinghurst Theatre Company: *Overflow* (for which she won the 2024 Time Out Sydney Critics Choice and People's Choice Awards); for Michael Louis Kennedy: *All The Fraudulent Horse Girls*; for White Box Theatre and Hasemann, Ball & Radda: *Mercury Fur*. Her screen credits include: for ABC: *Plum, Reef Break*; for Paramount+: *Last King of the Cross*.

Janet is also a changemaker and vocal advocate for transgender rights, she has written op-eds for Vogue, Fashion Journal and been interviewed for the ABC.

ABOUT GRIFFIN

Griffin is the only theatre company in the country exclusively devoted to the development and staging of new Australian writing. Located in the historic SBW Stables Theatre, nestled in the heart of Kings Cross, Griffin has been Australia's home for the exploration of new stories since 1979.

We are the launch pad for new plays, ideas and writing that other theatres won't take a risk on. We boldly contribute to Australia's unique and powerful storytelling culture. Plays like *Prima Facie, Holding the Man* and *City of Gold* all had their world premieres at Griffin before going out to capture the national imagination. In the words of our longest-serving Artistic Director, Ros Horin:

"We are the theatre of first chances."

We are passionate about nurturing emerging and established practitioners alike. We pride ourselves on supporting our vast community of artists, audiences and supporters who consider our theatre their creative home. We help ambitious, bold, risk-taking and urgent Australian work get from the page onto the stage. We tell the stories that help us know who we are as a nation, and who we want to become.

Acknowledgement of Country

Griffin Theatre Company operates and tells stories on the unceded lands of the Gadigal of the Eora Nation. We acknowledge and honour Aboriginal and Torres Strait Islander people as the oldest continuous living culture on the planet, with more than 60,000 years of storytelling practice shaping and underpinning all aspects of Australian culture. It is a privilege that we do not take lightly: to work on this land, and to tell stories on its soil.

GRIFFIN THEATRE COMPANY
13 Craigend St
Gadigal Land, Kings Cross, NSW 2011

CONTACT
02 9332 1052
info@griffintheatre.com.au
griffintheatre.com.au

GRIFFIN FAMILY

Board
Bruce Meagher (Chair)
Guillaume Babille
Nigel Barrington
Simon Burke AO
Julieanne Campbell
Jane Clifford
Declan Greene
Julia Pincus
Lenore Robertson AM
Simone Whetton

Artistic Director & Co-CEO
Declan Greene

Executive Director & Co-CEO
Julieanne Campbell

General Manager
Khym Scott

Associate Artistic Director
Anthea Williams

Literary Associate
Daley Rangi

Producer, *SISTREN*
Bali Padda

Head of Development
Jake Shavikin

Marketing Manager
Erica Penollar

Marketing & Content Producer
Christie Yip

Ticketing Manager
Gavin Roach

Front of House Manager
Alex Bryant-Smith

Front of House
Riordan Berry
Kathryn Collins
Max Philips
Maddy Withington
Willo Young

Administrator
Blake Hahn

Production Manager
Jimi Rawlings

Production & Technical Coordinator
Amy Norton

Finance Manager
Chrissy Riley

Finance Consultant
Emma Murphy

Publicity
Kabuku PR

Graphic Design
Paper Moose
Susu Studio

Cover Photography
Brett Boardman

ABOUT BELVOIR ST THEATRE

Belvoir St Theatre is a theatre company on a side street in Surry Hills, Sydney.

We share our street with a park and a public housing estate, and our theatre is in an old industrial building. It has been, at various times, a garage, a sauce factory, and the Nimrod Theatre. When the theatre was threatened with redevelopment in 1984, over 600 likeminded theatre-lovers formed a syndicate to buy the building and save it from becoming an apartment block. More than thirty years later, Belvoir continues to be at the forefront of Australian acting and storytelling for the stage. In 2026, that story takes a new turn. While Griffin Theatre Company's home is being redeveloped, Belvoir's Downstairs will be its temporary base. Two companies that care deeply about new Australian theatre, sharing a space with decades of creative history behind it and plenty more to come.

At Belvoir we gather the best theatre artists we can find, emerging and established, to realise an annual season of works – new works, both Australian and international, reimagined classics and a lasting commitment to Indigenous stories. Audiences remember many landmark productions including *Counting and Cracking, The Drover's Wife, Angels in America, Brothers Wreck, The Glass Menagerie, Neighbourhood Watch, The Wild Duck, Medea, The Diary of a Madman, Death of a Salesman, The Blind Giant is Dancing, Hamlet, Cloudstreet, Aliwa, The Book of Everything, Keating!, The Exile Trilogy, Exit the King, The Sapphires, Faith Healer, FANGIRLS, The Jungle and the Sea* and many more.

Today, under Artistic Director Eamon Flack and Executive Director Aaron Beach, Belvoir tours nationally and internationally, and continues to create its own brand of rough magic for new generations of audiences. We are proud to be creating work that speaks to life and experience in Australia and abroad, continuing our commitment to deliver diverse stories to diverse audiences. Belvoir receives government support for its activities from the federal government through the Australia Council and the state government through Create NSW. We also receive philanthropic and corporate support, which we greatly appreciate and welcome.

BELVOIR ST THEATRE

Gadigal Country
25 Belvoir St, Surry Hills, NSW 2010
belvoir.com.au

CONTACT

Box Office: +61 (2) 9699 3444
Administration: +61 (2) 9698 3344
mail@belvoir.com.au

BELVOIR ST THEATRE STAFF

DIRECTORS

Artistic Director
Eamon Flack

Executive Director
Aaron Beach

ARTISTIC & PROGRAMMING

Artistic Associate
Tom Wright

Resident Director
Hannah Goodwin

Resident Artist
Margaret Thanos

Literary Associate
Ayah Tayeh

Andrew Cameron Fellow
Mehhma Mahli

Balnaves Foundation Fellow
Hannah Belanszky
Bianca Hunt

PRODUCING

Head of Producing
Simone Parrott

Producer
Brittany Santargia

Artistic Administrator
Kelsey Martin

EA & ADMINISTRATION

Executive Assistant
Danielle Green

EDUCATION

Head of Education
Jane May

Education Coordinator
Nicola Denton

PRODUCTION

Head of Production
Tristan Ellis-Windsor

Production Manager
Ren Kenward

Deputy Production Manager
Dana Spence

Resident Stage Manager
Luke McGettigan

Costume Supervisor
Belinda Crawford

Technical Coordinator
Cameron Russell

Construction Manager
Darran Whatley

Leading Hand
Jonas Trovato

MARKETING & CUSTOMER SERVICE

Deputy Executive Director, Marketing, Community & People
Fiona Hulton

Box Office Manager
Natalie Elliot

CRM and Insights Manager
Jason Lee

Ticketing Systems Specialist & CRM Administrator
Tanya Ginori-Cairns

Box Office Coordinator
Lily Emerson

Marketing Manager
Laura Wallace

Digital Content Coordinator
Breanna Macey

Communications Administrator
Jessica Shoppee

Front of House Manager
Alison Benstead

PUBLICITY

Kabuku PR

DEVELOPMENT

Head of Development
Bernie Witham

Partnerships & Grants Manager
Lily O'Harte

Philanthropy Manager
Matt Skyes

Philanthropy Administrator
Ellen Harvey

FINANCE & OPERATIONS

Chief Financial Officer
Ash Rathod

Management Accountant
Jay Purohit

Financial Accountant
Dev Solanki

Finance Administrator
Shyleja Paul

BELVOIR ST THEATRE

Gadigal Country
25 Belvoir St, Surry Hills, NSW 2010
belvoir.com.au

CONTACT

Box Office: +61 (2) 9699 3444
Administration: +61 (2) 9698 3344
mail@belvoir.com.au

GRIFFIN DONORS

Income from Griffin activities covers less than 40% of our operating costs—leaving an ever-increasing gap for us to fill through government funding, sponsorship and the generosity of our individual supporters. Your support helps us bridge the gap and keep ticket prices affordable and our work at its best.

To make a donation and a difference, contact Griffin on **(02) 9332 1052** *or donate online at* **griffintheatre.com.au**

PROGRAM PATRONS

Griffin Ambassadors
Robertson Foundation

Griffin Amplify
Girgensohn Foundation

Griffin Literary Associate
Malcolm Robertson Foundation
Robertson Foundation

Griffin Redraft Fund
Shane & Cathryn Brennan

Suzie Miller Award
Suzie Miller

Griffin Studio
Gil Appleton
Darin Cooper Foundation
Corinne & Bryan
Kiong Lee & Richard Funston
Malcolm Robertson Foundation
Pip Rath & Wayne Lonergan
Geoff & Wendy Simpson AM
Danielle Smith & Sean Carmody

Griffin Studio Workshop
Shane & Cathryn Brennan (Patron)
Mary Ann Rolfe (Founding Patron)
Iolanda Capodanno
& Juergen Krufczyk
Darin Cooper Foundation
Corinne & Bryan
Bob & Chris Ernst
Jane-Maree Hurley
Susan MacKinnon
Jake Shavikin
Merilyn Sleigh & Raoul de Ferranti

Griffin Women's Initiative
Nicole Abadee
Katrina Barter
Simon Burke AO
Julieanne Campbell
Iolanda Capodanno
Jane Clifford
Jennifer Darin
Eveline Dowling
Mandy Foley
Nicola Forrest AO
Melinda Graham
Sherry Gregory
Rosemary Hannah
& Lynette Preston
Jane-Maree Hurley
Tessa Leong
Susan MacKinnon
Jane McDermott Austin
Suzie Miller
Naomi Parry
Julia Pincus
Ruth Ritchie
Lenore Robertson AM
Nawal Silfani
Ann Sloan
Deanne Weir
Simone Whetton
Anonymous (1)

PRODUCTION PARTNERS 2025

***Naturism* by Ang Collins**
Darin Cooper Foundation
Robert Dick & Erin Shiel
Mandy Foley
Rosemary Hannah
& Lynette Preston
Kate Morgan
Bruce Meagher & Greg Waters
Julia Pincus & Ian Learmonth

SEASON DONORS

Company Patrons $100,000+
Shane & Cathryn Brennan
Neilson Foundation

Season Patrons $50,000-$99,999
Malcolm Robertson Foundation
Robertson Foundation

Mainstage Donors $20,000-$49,999
Darin Cooper Foundation
Girgensohn Foundation
Rosemary Hannah
& Lynette Preston
Suzie Miller
Julia Pincus & Ian Learmonth
Sally Breen Family Foundation
Anonymous (1)

Production Donors $10,000-$19,999
Jenny Ainsworth
Carla Zampatti Foundation
Robert Dick & Erin Shiel
Doc Ross Family Foundation
Gordon & Marie Esden
Mandy Foley
Ingrid Kaiser
Bruce Meagher & Greg Waters
Kate Morgan
Mountain Air Foundation
Rebel Penfold-Russell OAM
Geoff & Wendy Simpson AM
The Skrzynski Foundation
The Wales Family Foundation
The WeirAnderson Foundation
Anonymous, in memory of
my daughter

Rehearsal Donors $5,000–$9,999
Brian Abel & Mark Manton
Antoinette Albert
Gil Appleton
Melissa Ball
Lisa Barker & Don Russell
Simon Burke AO
Margaret & Bernard Coles KC
Corinne & Bryan
Bob & Chris Ernst
Stephen Fitzgerald
Carrillo Gantner AC & Ziyin Gantner
Danny Gilbert AM & Kathleen Gilbert
Elizabeth Hurst
Lambert Bridge Foundation
Kiong Lee & Richard Funston
Polese Foundation
Pip Rath & Wayne Lonergan
Seaborn, Broughton & Walford
Foundation
Merilyn Sleigh & Raoul de Ferranti
Danielle Smith & Sean Carmody

Final Draft Donors $3,000–$4,999
Baly Douglass Foundation
Iolanda Capodanno
& Juergen Krufczyk
Sherry Gregory
John Head
Jane-Maree Hurley
Susan MacKinnon

GRIFFIN DONORS

Workshop Donors $1,000–$2,999
Nicole Abadee & Rob Macfarlan
Emily Aitken
Katrina Barter
Cherry & Peter Best
Ellen Borda
Ellen Borda
Helen Bowden
Stephen & Annabelle Burley
Julieanne Campbell
Anna Cleary
Jane Clifford
Max Dingle OAM
Eveline Dowling
Ari Droga
Toby Duffy
Brian Everingham
John & Libby Fairfax
Nicholas & Rowena Falzon
Sandra & Rupert Ferman
Sandra Forbes
Melinda Graham
Peter Graves Canberra
Reg Graycar
Mink Greene
Lisa Hamilton & Rob White
Kate Harrison
Libby Higgin & Gae Anderson
Mark Hopkinson & Michelle Opie
David Hoskins & Paul McKnight
Susan Hyde
Colleen Kane
Adrienne & David Kitching
Tessa Leong
John Lewis
Helen Lochhead AO
Patricia Lynch
Matthew & Josephine
Sandra & Kent McPhee
Jane McDermott Austin
Naomi Parry
Ian Phipps
Andrew Post & Susan Quill
Kate Richardson & Chris Marrable
Steve Riethoff
In memory of Katherine Robertson
Sylvia Rosenblum
Jake Shavikin
Nawal Silfani
Jann Skinner
Ann & Quinn Sloan
Geoffrey Starr
Arahni Sont
Leslie Stern
Martyn Thompson
Sue Thomson
Samantha Turley & Diego Silva
Janet Wahlquist
Richard Weinstein
& Richard Benedict
Simone Whetton
Anonymous (7)

Reading Donors $500–$999
Sally Beath
Alex Bowen & Catherine Sullivan
Alex Bryant-Smith
Jane Christensen
Nick & Carol Dettmann
Elizabeth Evatt
Peter Fogarty & Priscilla Adey
Erica Gray
Susi Hamilton
James Hartwright & Kerrin D'Arcy
Michael Jackson
Noella Lopez
Robert Marks
Simon Marrable
Christopher Matthies
& Graham Parsons
Siobahn Mullany
Jenni Neary AM
Belinda Piggott & David Ojerholm
Virginia Pursell
A.O. Redmond
Steph Sands
Patricia Spinks
Adam Suckling
Fiona Thomas
Stuart Thomas
Michael Thompson OAM & Ian Kelly
Duncan Thomson
Julie Whitfield
Anonymous (4)

First Draft Donors $200-$499
Robyn Ayres
Edwina Birch
Caitlin Brass
David Caulfield
Sue Clark
Edward Cooper & Daniel Zucker
Joanne Court
Brendan Crotty
Bryan Cutler
Melita Daru
Rosemary Dermody
Peter & Lou Duerden
Paul & Jean Eagar
Kevin Farmer
Yvonne Fetherston
R Furley
Deane Golding
Peter Gray & Helen Thwaites
Wendy Gray
Sue Halloran & Jim Allen
Matthew Huxtable
Marian & Nabeel Ibrahim
David Lacey
Bronwyn Leece
Liz Locke
George & Maruschka Loupis
Duncan McKay
Dr Stephen McNamara
Margaret Murphy
Dian Neligan
Carolyn Newman
Sally Patten
Peter Pezzutti
Meredith Phelps
Nick Read
Ann Rocca
Michael & Noelleen Rosen
David Russell
Kevin & Shirley Ryan
Erandi Samarakoon
Jane S
Margaret Teh
Rosemary White
Yoda & Modgie
William Zappa
Ray Ziesing
Anonymous (14)

Griffin Friends Forever
We remember and honour those who have generously supported the future of Australian storytelling through a bequest to Griffin Theatre Company.

Thank you:
Annette Mary Lunney
Estate of the Late John William Roe

CURRENT AS OF 27 MARCH 2026

GRIFFIN SPONSORS

Griffin would like to thank the following:

OUR PARTNERS

GOVERNMENT SUPPORTERS

PATRON

LEGACY BENEFACTOR

VENUE PARTNER

CREATIVE PARTNERS

SUSU STUDIO

COPYRIGHT AGENCY
CULTURAL FUND

GIRGENSOHN
FOUNDATION

ROBERTSON
FOUNDATION

COMPANY PARTNERS

All Things
All Creatures

bourke street bakery

FOUR PILLARS

MARQUE
LAWYERS

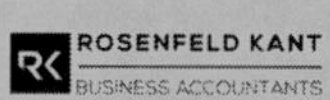

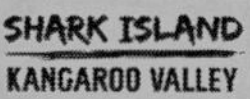

Griffin Theatre Company is assisted by the Australian Government through Creative Australia, its principal arts investment and advisory body.

Griffin Theatre Company is supported by the NSW Government through Create NSW.